JANUA LINGUARUM

STUDIA MEMORIAE
NICOLAI VAN WIJK DEDICATA

Series Critica 5

edenda curat

WERNER WINTER

LINGUISTIC STYLISTICS

by

NILS ERIK ENKVIST

1973

MOUTON

THE HAGUE · PARIS

LIBRARY OF CONGRESS CATALOG CARD NUMBER: 72–88182

Printed in Hungary

For Kjell, Kristian, and Elisabeth

PREFACE

My aim was to attempt a concise, introductory, and general inventory of current problems in linguistic stylistics, all within some 160 pages. Such a project suggests a number of decisions on policy of which the reader ought to be warned in advance.

To discuss all the various concepts and theories of stylistics that have been proposed, even in the past decade or two, would at once explode the limits of a small book. I have therefore frankly adopted a basic view of style as a differential between a text and a contextually related norm. Within this general frame I have, however, tried to mention a number of different, and sometimes conflicting, approaches. I have avoided voicing my own opinions about a host of controversies where such opinions did not seem necessary for my immediate purpose. For instance, I suggest that the description of style is not tied to any single grammatical model, though many of these models have virtues that other models lack.

Another problem is exemplification. The illustration and description of actual and potential style markers in different languages would have needed many times the space of the present essay. For concrete examples readers will therefore have to consult works listed in the references and in the bibliography. Nor have I tried to give anything like a full review of the enormous body of stylistic research available in the major European languages alone. My bias has been frankly in favour of English.

I doubt that anybody can honestly claim to master all the research into stylistics in all the world's languages. My own references have been picked from among the works I have come across during several years of fairly comprehensive reading. At several points I touch upon matters general enough to warrant very long lists of references. Such lists were omitted as impracticable and not very helpful. The bibliography does, however, include a number of works not referred to in the text. Some are general and bear on many relevant questions; others are specific, and their relevance should appear from their titles.

My debts of gratitude are numerous enough to defy brief listing. Most of the arguments have been tried on generations of students at Åbo Akademi as well as at several other universities in various countries. Many queries and discussions have helped to define problems, though not always to solve them. My most concrete debts are to Professor I. R. Galperin, Dr. Hakan Ringbom, Lector Geoffrey Phillips, and Lector Kurt Johansson. To Professor Werner Winter and Miss Swantje Koch I owe thanks for friendly editing, and to my family for patience and encouragement while I was writing beside a heavy load of teaching and administration. Travel grants from the Academy of Finland and from the H. W. Donner Fund and Swedish Jubilee Fund of Åbo Akademi enabled me to look up references abroad.

The manuscript was completed in February, 1971.

Åbo Akademi
20500 Åbo 50, Finland
February, 1971   N.E.E.

CONTENTS

1

INTRODUCTION

1.1 DOES STYLE EXIST?

STYLE is a concept as common as it is elusive: most of us speak about it, even lovingly, though few of us are willing to say precisely what it means. Those who write vaguely, subjectively, and impressionistically about it remain open to charges of conceptual looseness, however elegantly they may express their prejudices. Yet those who spend their energies on rigorous definitions of style and who support their statements with exact facts and figures fare no better. They have often been ridiculed for tortuous pedantry and chastised for breaking butterflies on the wheel.

Far fewer are those who deny the very existence of style. Indeed most people have accepted a tacit, ontological argument: the fact that the idea of style is so widespread and so useful proves that there is an objective entity underlying this idea. 'So many people cannot be wrong' has been one of the silent tenets of many a stylistician's creed.

Ontological proofs can, however, be refuted just as readily as they can be upheld. The most recent attempt at refutation comes from Bennison GRAY, and his argument should be briefly rehearsed to start us off (GRAY 1969). GRAY's central question is, Does style in fact exist at all? His answer is a vigorous negative. Style, he says, is like the emperor's clothes or the ether of old physics. It exists merely because people want to see it because everybody else does, or perhaps because it buries a number of mysteries under a handy, respectable term. In GRAY's opinion it hides a vacuity that more thorough research would be bound to reveal.

GRAY supports his contention by trying to refute one approach to style after another. If we study style as behaviour in the manner of the psychologist, he says, we in fact study character, personality, or individuality. Therefore we should say so and not pretend to be working with style. If, in the rhetorician's manner, we identify style with the speaker, we assume that a man's language has a physiognomic relation to the man himself. But this must be proved, not assumed. If we turn philologists and study style as the 'latent' in the manner of Leo SPITZER, we are in fact studying subject matter:

The lesson of Spitzer's fifty years of application to the problem of style is that he could not succeed in distinguishing style from the work, or, if you will, structure from content. (GRAY 1969: 62)

But — alas — those who define style as the individual, and thus become literary critics, fare no better. For individuality, says GRAY, is not a matter of style but of language, subject matter, content, theme, and referent. Indeed the collocation *individual style* is a needless tautology: if we can recognise a given writer's work, we do so not by 'style' but by a total pattern. This view of style as the individual element is but another aspect of an exaltation of romantic originality. Nor do we solve our problem if we define style as an 'implicit speaker'. GRAY reminds us how Professor WIMSATT once defined stylistic judgments as comparisons of what a writer had said with what he ought to have said, but nevertheless later subscribed to the theory of the intentional fallacy (WIMSATT 1941, 1954). One might, however, reply that comparing a text with an imaginary norm does not involve any reference to the author's intentions. The norm is rather set up by the critic.

So far, a linguist might be tempted to nod in at least partial agreement. But GRAY uses the same Occamist razor to slash at linguists as well. To begin with, he says, linguists live in

the realm of the about-to-be-established. Nor is style as choice
— a favourite linguistic notion — a workable concept, because
we can never know what choices in fact were available to a
particular author. And how can we define choice in linguistic
terms? To hedge behind 'synonymy' by defining style as
choice between items that mean the same is not a satisfactory
solution. If two words are synonyms, there is no difference
between them. If they are not, the difference is one of meaning, and the term *style* is once again superfluous. GRAY sums
up:

In every case of the use of the word 'style' which we have examined,
the user has found it necessary to go outside the work to establish
the existence of style, and in every case he has had to go to something
for which there exists no evidence but the particular work whose
style he wishes to discuss. (GRAY 1969: 107)

GRAY is a diehard organicist: to him a literary work is one
and indivisible, without dichotomies between content and
form, style and expression, process and result. His scepticism
is bent on reducing terms and concepts to a minimum. If we
can do without the concept of 'style' we must discard it at
once, he insists. But does this necessarily follow? One might
agree with GRAY that it is our duty to define precisely what
we mean by *style*, and still insist that the term is a convenient
abbreviation, precisely as 'horse-power' is a useful concept
for 'a unit measuring the work of a prime motor taken as
equalling 550 foot-pounds per second', or as 'yellow' is handier
than 'the most luminous primary colour occurring in the
spectrum between green and orange'. Philosophers of science
have dwelt on this difference between SUBSTANTIVE TERMS
and NOTATIONAL TERMS. Substantive terms are irreplaceable
without loss of conceptual content, whereas notational terms
are, basically, abbreviations and can thus be paraphrased
(KAPLAN 1964: 49). All the same, even notational terms are
useful and may even be necessary. There is no reason to ban
the term *style* even if it were notational, not substantive, as

long as we remember that notational terms must always be defined with the aid of more basic concepts.

As to the organic view, one may indeed admit that both meaning and aesthetic effect may be regarded as the sum total of everything that goes into a text, including the "style" of that text, in whatever terms it be defined. But one may still insist that texts must be analysed and taken apart into components by various methods, and that the quest for correlations between the effect of the whole work and the individual stimuli and their combinations in the text that caused this response is a highly legitimate procedure. Indeed the business of literary criticism might be defined as such a quest.

1.2 STYLE AS A NOTATIONAL TERM.
STYLE AS DEPARTURE, ADDITION, AND CONNOTATION

Many scholars have felt that *style* is a notational term and therefore tried to give us stringent definitions. Some have even tried to botanize in the flora of such paraphrases (DeVito 1967, Enkvist – Spencer – Gregory 1964, Sayce 1962). A taxonomy of definitions might be based on a number of principles. Thus some students of style have concentrated on the relations between the speaker/writer and the text, and thus found clues to style mainly in the personality and environment of the people who have generated the text. Others have focussed their interest on the relations between the text and the listener/reader, often pointing out that the receiver's reactions to textual stimuli are more readily accessible to study than are the generative impulses that motivated the sender of the message. If so, the study of style now becomes based on the recipient's responses to certain features in the text. A third group of investigators have tried to objectify the approach and to eliminate references to the communicants at either end of the communication process. They look for clues to style in descriptions of the text, not in appeals to personalities. This necessitates the use of objective methods, not least to distinguish the stylistically significant features of a text from the non-stylistic ones.

Along another dimension it has been suggested that all linguistic views of style tend to be based on one of three fundamentally different views. First, style can be seen as a DEPARTURE from a set of patterns which have been labelled as a NORM *(style comme écart)*. According to this principle, stylistic analysis turns out to consist of comparisons between features in the text whose style we wish to analyse, and features in the body of text that we have defined as a norm and therefore regard as a relevant background. Secondly, style has been viewed as an ADDITION of certain stylistic traits to a neutral, styleless, or prestylistic expression. If so, stylistic analysis becomes a stripping process in which we peel off, isolate, and describe the stylistic skin and meat that surround the stylistically neutral or unmarked core. Conversely, in the generation of texts, the speaker/writer is supposed to start from a prestylistic or stylistically neutral or unmarked core of meaning, which he then surrounds with a halo of style. Thirdly, style has been viewed as CONNOTATION, whereby each linguistic feature acquires its stylistic value from the textual and situational environment. Stylistic analysis therefore becomes a study of the relations between specific linguistic units and their environment.

But these three approaches may also be seen as complementary rather than as contradictory or mutually exclusive. If we define a relevant norm against which we match our text, and if we thus succeed in isolating those departures from the norm that have stylistic significance, we seem to be applying the first of the three methods. If, however, the norm is regarded as STYLISTICALLY NEUTRAL or UNMARKED, the same comparison also satisfies the requirements of the second definition: the features by which the text differs from the norm are then identical with those by which a stylistically marked text differs from a stylistically unmarked, neutral norm. And if we

define the norm, not on grounds of general relevance or of
stylistic neutrality but expressly with the aid of definite CON-
TEXTUAL RELATIONSHIPS which justify the comparison of text
and norm, we are in fact also viewing style as connotation.
We are defining stylistically significant features in terms of
contextual, that is, textual and situational, environment.

1.3 TYPES OF LINGUISTIC VARIATION

Linguists are, of course, only one of the groups that are
interested in the styles of language. Linguistics might be
defined as that branch of learning which builds models of
texts and languages on the basis of theories of language, and
which evaluates the success of such models with the aid of
explicit criteria. It is the task of LINGUISTIC STYLISTICS, or
STYLOLINGUISTICS, to set up inventories and descriptions of
stylistic stimuli with the aid of linguistic concepts. One might
add at once that practical work in stylolinguistics may be, but
need not be, an exercise in its own right. Stylolinguistic
analyses may be directed towards goals beyond linguistics
proper. They may, for instance, be a first step in a wider,
structural, literary, and historical study of a text or a
language.

By definition, linguists should be interested in all kinds of
LINGUISTIC VARIATION. And style is only one of many types
of such variation. Other types are TEMPORAL, REGIONAL, and
SOCIAL DIALECT, as well as IDIOLECT and REGISTER. A linguistic
form is temporal if it correlates with a given period. The
English of the Authorized Version of the Bible, for instance,
represents an earlier stage in the history of the language.
Linguistic forms whose occurrences correlate with areas on a
map are definable as regional dialects, or dialects for short.
And those whose occurrences correlate with the social class
of their users are social dialects, or SOCIOLECTS. As we saw
above, one way of defining styles is to regard them as varia-

tions that correlate with contexts and situations. Some linguists prefer the term REGISTER for types of language that correlate with situation, and use the term *style* to indicate individual variation within each register. Others have reserved *register* for the different subtypes of language that people use when acting in different social roles: thus a doctor uses one register in the operating theatre, another with a patient, and a third when playing with his children. The term IDIOLECT is often used to indicate the language of one individual, usually in its totality. Actually the terminology varies among different schools of linguists and even with individual linguists within each school. One useful term is LINGUISTIC DIATYPE, which covers all the different subvarieties of language mentioned above.

1.4 OVERLAP OF STYLISTICS AND OTHER BRANCHES OF LINGUISTICS

Unless stated otherwise, the term *style* will here be reserved for that type of linguistic variation which correlates with context in a wide sense of the term, including both textual context and situational context. But as *style* is a notational term rather than a linguistic prime, it should be emphasized that other definitions and terminologies are possible and perhaps even plausible. There is nothing to prevent readers who so desire from translating the substance and models of this book's argument into the terminology of their own preference.

Such translation may be motivated not only by the notational character of the term *style*, but also by the obvious fact that the different categories of linguistic variation overlap. The English of the 1611 Bible is a temporal variant of English, but at the same time a living style of twentieth-century English which must be included in a full inventory of current stylistic variants. Innumerable examples could be cited of situations in which regional dialect correlates not only with region but also with social class: for instance, upper-class people may speak a supraregional standard language, whereas lower-class people use regionally definable dialects. And if, as often happens, there are people who speak standard language in one type of situation and a *patois* or regional dialect in another type of situation, the use of regional dialect thus comes to correlate with situation and the dialect becomes a style. In a similar manner, sociolects may assume the function of styles, for instance if a speaker uses upper-class language in one type of situation and lower-class language in another. There are many societies in which situational correlations exist even for the choice of language. Thus languages such as Latin, French, English, Russian, and Hindi have often ousted various vernaculars from certain contexts such as scientific or administrative communication, and in societies characterized by DIGLOSSIA the choice of language is contextually conditioned. Thus higher variants such as Classical Arabic and *katharevusa* are used in sermons, formal speeches, and lectures, whereas the lower variants such as colloquial Arabic and *dhimotiki* occur in instructions to workmen and in familiar conversation. (GUMPERZ 1966, FERGUSON 1966, DENISON 1969) In societies with many immigrants, varying patterns of language loyalty may also lead to a bilingualism, or even multilingualism, in which languages assume the context-determined role of styles (FISHMAN 1966). Where such situations exist, we may view the use of a language in the function of a style as another of the many instances of rank shift that occur in language.

In this light, our terminology of linguistic subtypes must be determined by our aims and perspectives. It is relative rather than absolute. Of course the examination of all these overlaps is relevant to stylistics as well as to other branches of language study. In our description of styles it is important to note for example that a person's formal style consists of, say, a supra-dialectal, non-regional standard, whereas his familiar style is a regional or social variant. We must accept the fact that stylistics often intersects other areas of linguistics: historical linguistics, dialectology, and sociolinguistics. But the choice of conceptual frame and terminology must fit the purpose and approach of each investigation. Therefore, different branches of language study ought to be regarded not as rivals but as different sets of tools, each of which may have its own advantages in a particular job. We should choose the one that works best. Thus it becomes idle to argue whether a given type of language is a temporal, regional, social, or stylistic variant. It should perhaps be given more labels than one. To the historian of English, *thou lovest* is an older form than *you love;* to the student of contemporary styles, it is a feature of a style that one might label as 'Biblical' or 'archaic'. To those who find *you ain't* characteristic of a social class it is a CLASS MARKER, but to those in whose studies it correlates with a certain range of situations it becomes a STYLE MARKER. In a full study of linguistic variation, both observations may be equally relevant. (Cf. ELLIS – URE 1968, GREGORY 1967, LABOV 1966, LOMAN 1970, URE 1968.)

Such overlaps can be very complicated, not least in assessments of the style of old texts. One example of such a complication was cited by RIFFATERRE in connection with the contrast between French *réussite* and *heureux succès*. Today, *réussite* is stylistically more neutral, *heureux succès* archaic. In the seventeenth century, however, *réussite* was a bold neologism readily spotted as a borrowing of Italian *riuscita* (RIFFATERRE 1959). Such changes in, and crossovers of, stylistic values pose a *caveat* to all readers of old texts, while also showing the relevance of historical, diachronic perspectives even in apparently synchronic stylistics.

Many sociolinguistic studies are of great importance for students of style as well. For instance in William LABOV's sophisticated study of the social strata of English in New York City (LABOV 1966), a number of observations concern correlations between language and situation. Thus LABOV found

that many New Yorkers tend to use postvocalic r more often
in formal than in informal contexts, while at the same time
the frequency of postvocalic r could be used to rank people
on a social scale. For example,

A professor of sociology born and raised in New York City began a
lecture with an (E) index of 50 to 60; as he proceeded and warmed
to his subject, the index dropped precipitately, as low as (r) —05;
then as he began to make his final points, the (r) index began to rise
again, though it never quite reached its initial value. A Negro woman,
living on welfare in a bare tenement apartment, used a carefully
articulated style of speech with (r) —19; now and then she interrupted
herself to scold her children, using a radically different style of speech
with (r) —00. (LABOV 1966: 56-7)

This suggests that both the professor and the Negro woman
had two styles, one more formal and one less formal, and each
consisted of a sociolect marked by a certain frequency of postvocalic r. Another of the categories of sociolinguistic investigation that have obvious stylistic importance is that dealing
with the choice of pronouns and modes of address (e.g.
LAMBERT 1967).

1.5 STYLE, GENRE, FUNCTION

Altogether, one scholar's style may be another scholar's
dialect, historical form, sociolect, or even language. As
Werner WINTER has noted, stylistics may profit from such
overlaps by borrowing methods from well-developed areas of
linguistics such as dialectology (WINTER 1964). In literary
study, too, certain concepts are highly useful in stylolinguistic
description. Thus there is a very close relationship between
style and GENRE, if genre is defined as 'a culturally definable,
traditional type of communication'. A genre could then be
regarded as a culturally definable stable context category —
or stable cluster of contextual features — which usually
correlates to some extent with a certain style, that is, with

a certain type of language. Also, the connection between genre and function of language is a close one. If we identify genre with linguistic function, GENRE STYLES such as the styles of poetry, scientific communication, journalism, and colloquial conversation become FUNCTIONAL STYLES. This presupposes the setting-up of correlations between traditional genres and those constellations of contextual features that we like to define as FUNCTIONS OF LANGUAGE. In fact, terms such as *genre* and *function* also turn out to be notational terms rather than linguistic primes. They are shorthand labels for various combinations of contextual primes. For example, in a certain social setting, both poetry and journalism may share the feature 'written', whereas the feature 'metrical' may be characteristic of poetry alone. This is worth noting because if we can develop a frame for the description and classification of contextual features, we may also use it for the classification of genres and functions in the sense of culturally definable, traditional uses of language.

1.6 STYLE AS COMPARISON AND PREDICTION

Even if style is defined as that variety of language which correlates with context, including situation, the recognition and analysis of styles are squarely based on comparison. The essence of variation, and thus of style, is difference, and differences cannot be analysed and described without comparison.

Comparisons are also necessary to show ranges of linguistic variation in specific situations. Situational correlations do not always operate with hundred-per-cent certainty. In fact, strong stylistic effects are often created precisely by departing from the usage that is customary in the situation involved. The effect becomes strong because it thwarts the recipient's expectations. If, for instance, a clergyman indulges in slang and in four-letter words in a high-church sermon, his audience is likely to be shocked. And if a corporal addresses a squad of recruits on the barrack square in the language usually associated with sermons, the effect will also be remarkable. In each situation, the recipient of a message — provided that he knows the language and is familiar with the situation — will expect that message to be couched in a certain type of situation-bound language. When the message emerges, the expectations are fulfilled or disappointed to varying degrees. If the expectations are fulfilled, the message has conformed to the style usually associated with that situation: the message has a high stylistic predictability, a HIGH STYLISTICITY. If they are disappointed, the message departs from the usual style and has LOW STYLISTICITY.

There are several corollaries to this simple principle. One has to do with the range of variation characteristic of each situation. There are contexts in which language is very highly formalized: military commands, greetings, legal formulae, and ritual language in general. Such "FROZEN" LANGUAGE (Joos 1962) can also occur in everyday situations, for instance around the breakfast table. There are other contexts which are characterized by very wide ranges of variation, like modern poetry. In fact the RANGE OF LINGUISTIC VARIATION in a given situation may itself turn into a characteristic of style: certain styles allow far wider variation than others.

Another basic aspect of stylistic comparison emerges out of the well-known fact that different people may react differently to the style of a given text. Their reactions depend on what they expect of it, that is, what norm they choose to compare it with. Now the choice of norm is conditioned by past experience of language in context. Even a native speaker cannot be conversant with all the styles of his language. Therefore people with different backgrounds will often react differently to one and the same text: their stores of past experience and their norms are different. And even people with a similar background may, consciously or subconsciously, choose to match a given text against different norms. One of the traditional aims of literary education has been to make students conversant with a body of recommended texts embodying a set of styles, and thus stylistic norms, against which they can match the texts they meet. In foreign-language teaching, one of the tasks necessary before the student achieves near-native command of the foreign language is to expose him to a suitably selected range of language variants, including situational ones, with which he can compare other texts and which he can use as a diagnostic frame for the recognition of styles. As we shall see below in section *8.1.2,* these problems also appear in stylostatistical comparisons of texts.

When we compare two texts, we may find that a linguistic feature occurs in one text but not in the other. It may be more frequent in one than in the other. Or it may have roughly the same frequency in both. In each of these three possible cases we are involved with FREQUENCIES, greater or smaller, including zero frequency (which is the same as non-occurrence). And if we reckon with the length of the text when assessing the frequencies, we should more properly speak about DEN-SITIES of linguistic features, the density of a given feature being definable as its number of occurrences divided with a measure for the length of the text, such as the number of running words.

If the densities of certain features are appreciably different in the two texts — which we might label as TEXT and NORM, the text being the text we study and the norm the body of texts against which we match our text, or the body of expectations based on past experience — these features are STYLE MARKERS, that is, stylistically significant features. If, again, the density of a given feature is roughly the same in text and norm, that feature is, in terms of this comparison, stylistically unmarked or neutral — that is, equally characteristic of both text and norm. It should perhaps be repeated once again that the results of such comparisons are entirely dependent on the choice of norm: if two people match the same text against different norms, their impressions of its style will be different. In the evaluation of literary texts, very often new norms are brought to bear on a classic text.

As I have argued elsewhere (ENKVIST – SPENCER – GREGORY 1964), if this reasoning is pursued further, it will lead to a definition of style based on comparison between text and norm. In ordinary communication, people who know the language do not choose just any norm for comparison with a text: the norm chosen must have a definite CONTEXTUAL RELATIONSHIP with the text. If we read a sonnet, we are more likely to compare it with other sonnets than with, say, a telephone book or a newspaper article. The impression of style, then, arises out of a comparison of the densities of linguistic features in the text with the densities of the corresponding linguistic features in a contextually related norm. If we view the same process, not as a comparison between a static text and a static norm but as a continuous matching of a linear, emerging text with a set of expectations conditioned by past experience, we may rephrase the definition in terms of expectations, or, better, probabilities. The style of a text thus becomes the aggregate of the contextual probabilities of linguistic features. Such probabilities may be studied either with the aid of informants — RIFFATERRE (1959) suggested the concept 'AR' or 'average reader' — or through computation of densities of linguistic features in text and norm. Those who desire concrete illustrations of stylistic analysis with the aid of density comparisons and contextual probabilities may, for instance, consult statistical studies of author identification such as those by ELLEGÅRD (1962a, 1962b) or MOSTELLER — WALLACE (1963, 1964). Such studies are based precisely on computations of significant differences in the densities of linguistic features in a text and in a contextually related norm.

If we agree to define style as the result of a comparison of densities of linguistic features in a text and a contextually related though suitably contrasting norm, we have at the same time covered a wide range of problems sometimes regarded as separate branches of stylistics that are hard to fit under a single definition. The style of an individual will emerge out of a comparison of that individual's texts with a norm consisting of comparable texts but by other people. A study of the special characteristics of poetic styles would naturally begin by matching poems against non-poetic texts. The study of 'expressive' or 'emotive' features should start by matching texts containing such features against non-expressive or non-emotive texts, and so forth. If this argument is correct, all stylistic analysis will consist of matching a text against a norm. Different varieties of stylistics arise through variations in types of text and types of norm. And different results, including contradictory opinions of the style of one and the same text, may arise if different analysts match that text against different norms, all of which may be justified by definite contextual relationships with the text at hand.

1.7 SUMMARY

In this introduction, I began by noting that *style* is a notational term rather than a linguistic prime. That is, *style* is a term that can be defined in terms of other, more basic notions, some of which will be discussed in the following chapters. If styles are defined as those varieties of language that correlate with contexts, including both textual and situational envelopes, there will always be considerable overlap between them and a number of concepts of historical, geographical, and sociological linguistics. Stylolinguistics is thus one of the ways in which we may view language. A stylolinguist is concerned with the same linguistic features as others may wish to consider in other perspectives and describe with different terminologies. I have also argued once again that impressions of style always arise out of comparisons. We match the text against another body of texts which we might label as *norm*, this norm being chosen because it is contextually relevant as a background for the text. And this matching process will result in an assessment of the differences in the densities of linguistic features that make the text different from the norm. Features whose densities are significantly different in the text and in the norm are style markers for the text in relation to the norm used. A change of norm may result in a different inventory of style markers.

The norm may be chosen from a wide field. One portion of a text may be matched against other portions or the whole of the same text. One text may be compared to other texts. Or the text may be set against an imaginary norm that only exists in a critic's mind.

STYLE AND LITERARY STUDY

2.1 RELATIONS BETWEEN LINGUISTICS, STYLISTICS, AND LITERARY STUDY

I have already spoken for a view which frankly admits that stylolinguistics is merely one of several possible ways of looking at language. The features that one scholar may regard as stylistic may be labelled as historical, regional, or social variants by those who prefer to start out from different linguistic premises. But this is not all. Indeed there are many devotees of other disciplines who are vitally concerned with stylistic features and who wish to consider them from angles very different from that of the stylolinguist. Prominent among them are the students of literature. Literary traditions also perforce enter into stylolinguistics because they are part of the context that helps us to define the norm with which we compare our text. It is therefore relevant to survey the vexing question of the relationship between linguistics, stylistics, and that comprehensive *Literaturwissenschaft* which I shall here, for convenience, simply call LITERARY STUDY.

The relationship between these three disciplines can be set in different ways. We may, for instance, regard stylistics as a subdepartment of linguistics, and give it a special subsection dealing with the peculiarities of literary texts. We may choose to make stylistics a subdepartment of literary study which may on occasion draw on linguistic methods. Or we may regard stylistics as an autonomous discipline which draws freely, and eclectically, on methods both from linguistics and from literary study.

Each approach has its own virtues, and arguing for the general supremacy of one over another would be a futile exercise. Such arguments only become meaningful in specific instances: for a given task, one approach may be better than another. It is one thing to study styles as types of linguistic variation, and a very different thing to describe the style of one particular text for a literary purpose such as finding out where its author drew his inspiration. All the same, literary methods have so dominated stylistics that a brief list of some important schools of literary stylistics is indicated even in a book whose burden is on the linguistic side. Indeed the catalogue of literary schools that have contributed germinal ideas relevant to stylolinguistics is a long one. It comprises at least French *explication de texte*, the approaches of VOSSLER and CROCE and SPITZER, Russian formalism, the literary tenets of the Prague school, Anglo–American New Criticism with its various offshoots, and, most recently, French Neo-Structuralism.

2.2 CLOSE READING. VOSSLER, CROCE, SPITZER

Explication de texte has nineteenth-century roots. Its aim was a close reading which correlated historical and linguistic information and sought connections between aesthetic responses and specific stimuli in the text; its refusal to congeal into set patterns was both a strength and weakness. The New Criticism that began in Britain before World War II and became a dominant movement in British and American criticism in the post-war years shared this interest in the text. The important basis of criticism was the text, not the biography of the author or the history of his times. At best, the New Critics threw sharp light on poetic details, on technique and structure; at worst they worked in a cultural vacuum and ignored such features as could be understood only in elaborate reconstructions of their original, cultural, and linguistic setting. Obviously, the increase in attention to textual detail was apt to bring literary criticism closer to linguistics. Curiously enough, the gap between these two disciplines was not bridged, however — perhaps because contemporary linguists were preoccupied with small units such as phonemes and morphemes, which were particularly amenable to the methods of taxonomic structuralism. Some persons associated with New Criticism, notably I. A. RICHARDS, have made their mark in linguistics as well.

VOSSLER, CROCE, SPITZER, and other "idealists" tried different avenues to find the ideas underlying the surface of linguistic expression. VOSSLER was particularly interested in clues to national cultures behind linguistic details. CROCE regarded language as creation and therefore made linguistics a subdepartment of aesthetics. And SPITZER wrote his stimulating essays by allowing his famous literary sensibility to react to different types of features in a range of text and by giving his vast erudition free rein in tracing parallels between culture and expression. Linguists, who are brought up to use stringent and explicit methods, are tempted to find such studies lacking in methodological rigour. Indeed SPITZER himself was the first to emphasize that he had no method that could be precisely described. His approach — the SPITZERIAN CIRCLE — was first to spot stylistic stimuli by intuition, and then to offer such explanations as brought back the argument to its starting-point. SPITZER's own brilliance guaranteed a stock of norms against which he could meaningfully match his texts. But those who lack his insight are likely to be better served by more pedestrian and explicit methods.

2.3 RUSSIAN FORMALISM

The Russian formalists have not yet exhausted their role, partly because of the language barriers. In a sense they have been rediscovered in the past several years, not least thanks

to new translations (TODOROV 1965, STRIEDTER 1969), and
their impact for instance on the French Neo-Structuralists is
obvious. The origins of Russian formalism can be sought in a
protest against the academic preoccupation with linguistic
and literary history and against the symbolist movement.
During the early years of World War I, groups of brilliant
young scholars at Moscow and Petrograd crystallized the
formalist principles into a programme and began applying it
to a wide range of concrete problems. Their focus was on the
devices of artistry, not on content: the student of literature
was to concentrate on the 'how' rather than on the 'what'.
In stylistics, the formalists were the opposite pole from the
idealists. Though formalism remained a collection of individual ideas with a common background, not a monolithic
doctrine, and though stylistics meant different things to
different formalists, the centre of attention was always the
formal manifestation of styles. From CHRISTIANSEN's *Philosophie der Kunst* (1909) the formalists borrowed the principle
of *Differenzqualität*, through which qualities originate in a di-
vergence from a norm. Roman JAKOBSON began formulating
the distinction between artistic prose based on metonymy and
poetry based on metaphor; TYNJANOV studied relation between genres of poetry and the corresponding levels of speech;
ŽIRMUNSKIJ and EICHENBAUM adopted more inclusive views
of style which included composition as well as theme; and
VINOGRADOV analysed verbal reflections of motifs in key
words and word clusters, as well as relations between context
and language in texts such as Avvakum's seventeenth-century
autobiography (ERLICH 1969, LÉONT'ÉV 1968).

The Russian formalists thus commented on the relationship between style and context as well as on the character of
style as deviance from a norm. The movement, however,
declined, its very name became synonymous with official
opprobrium, and by about 1930 it had lost its first impetus.
Many of its principles have best survived in the works of the
Prague School. Still, even Soviet stylistics was continually

inspired by these beginnings. V. V. VINOGRADOV was one of those instrumental in defining the subsequent positions of Soviet stylistics. Stylistic analysis, he said, should view the literary text as a dialectical combination of elements at different levels, and thus not only at the formal level: ideas, themes, and literary structure are the forces shaping the linguistic surface of a text. Style concerns itself with organization at all levels, and linguistic stylistics is the subdepartment which studies such organization at the linguistic level. Therefore formal, linguistic stylistics is only one part of stylistics, and the study of literature is not merely a subdepartment of linguistics. VINOGRADOV has divided stylistics into three departments: linguistic or structural stylistics which operates with linguistic concepts; the stylistics of speech or *reč'* which deals with the characteristics of genres, groups of texts, and individual texts; and the stylistics of artistic literature whose highest form is the discovery of the aesthetic effects of structural features in a literary work. VINOGRADOV thus professed a certain antiformalism:

in its method of approach to the analysis of structures of verbal art, literary stylistics — a branch of the general stylistics of art — is dominated by the categories and concepts of philosophical aesthetics and literary theory (VINOGRADOV 1963: 205).

2.4 LITERARY STRUCTURALISM

Another line of influence runs from modern stylistics back to Vladimir PROPP's studies of the morphology of the folktale, also an important outgrowth of Russian formalism. PROPP noted that the plots of Russian folktales could be described in terms of combinations of discrete elements. He listed thirty-one thematic categories such as the theme of absence ('one of the members of a family is absent from home'), departure ('the hero leaves home'), interdiction ('the hero is forbidden something'), provision ('the hero is given a magic agent'), and

so on. Thus each folktale is no longer seen as a unique object
sui generis, but rather as a selection from, and combination
of, these universal themes or "functions". When the analytic
principle is extended to cover character, Russian folktales are
found to have seven types of *dramatis personae:* a villain, a
donor, a helper, a sought-for person, a dispatcher, a hero, and
a false hero. (PROPP 1958)

Such categories are more closely concerned with the structure of the literary work than directly with style. But if style
is defined as that kind of linguistic variation that correlates
with context, and if elements of literary structures such as
those of PROPP are viewed as contextual categories, they
become relevant to stylolinguistics as well. They give us a
more sensitive taxonomy of literary contexts than, say, rough
distinctions between dialogue and description.

The quest for such universals of narrative structure has
been more recently continued by BARTHES (1966), TODOROV
and others, and applied to some English themes by CHATMAN
(1969). According to one version of neo-structuralist theory,
narrative consists of story and discourse. The story is formed
by the action and by the characters, whereas the discourse
consists of the relations between narrator and reader such as
the time scale, the aspect, and the mode of the narrative. The
story can be split up into minimal narrative units called
functions. These functions combine into larger units or actions,
which together form the narrative. Functions are either kernels, that is branching points in the story in which choices
between alternative courses of behaviour take place, or
catalysts which merely elaborate a path of behaviour chosen
in a kernel. A third type of functions are the indices which do
not link a function to the events proper in the narrative but
which refer to character or atmosphere. Thus a description of
a knife in a person's belt is a catalyst if the knife is actually
used in the story, but remains an index if it merely illustrates
the appearance and character of its owner. Proportions
between kernels, catalysts, and indices can be regarded as

characteristics of a writer's narrative structure, and in that sense of his narrative style. But such universals might also be viewed as stylolinguistic context categories. They make it theoretically possible to study and contrast for instance the language of kernels and catalysts with the language of indices, and to find out whether a given writer might be said to have a different style for the expression of each of these functions.

2.5 LINGUISTIC *VERSUS* LITERARY CONTEXT

Thus various, sometimes very dogmatic, attitudes have been voiced about the relations between linguistics, stylistics, and literary study, and they have even acquired political overtones. In practical work, such problems tend to solve themselves pragmatically, as long as each investigator allows himself the freedom of choosing and shaping his methods as they best help him to achieve his own particular goals. In some studies, stylistics may be an auxiliary brought in to elucidate narrative structure; in others, categories of narrative structure provide contexts for stylistic analysis.

An example (ENKVIST 1964, CASSIRER 1970): In *The Doll's House*, Nora says: "I leave the keys here." As long as we limit ourselves to the linguistic garb of this utterance, we may content ourselves by noting that it is dressed up in everyday language which perfectly harmonizes with its domestic context. We must go into the dramatic structure of the play to notice that Nora's line in fact is a major kernel, as it signals Nora's determination to break with her past. To understand the full impact of an utterance, we must simultaneously analyse both its linguistic surface in terms of a linguistic context such as 'everyday middleclass conversation', and its meaning in terms of the context of narrative and action. Only thus can we note that an expression which, against one contextual background, seems trivial and highly predictable may carry a very great amount of information and thus be highly significant when seen in the light of another contextual background (here the structure of *The Doll's House*). How far we wish to go in our discussion of an utterance such as this will of course depend on our purpose. If we study Ibsen's Norwegian style in general, we may dismiss Nora's line as a trivial example of everyday dialogue. If, on the contrary, we study *The Doll's House* or the way in which Ibsen builds up a dramatic climax, we should carefully note the tension between a major narrative kernel and its undramatic expression. The apparatus developed by PROPP, BARTHES, TODOROV, and others is likely to be of use for those who wish to study correlations between narrative elements and their linguistic expression.

2.6 SUMMARY

Altogether: we may approach styles in more than one way. There is a basic distinction between mere linguistic description of stimuli that we have defined as stylistic, and a description not only of the stimuli themselves but also of their full narrative, semantic, and aesthetic effects. In the words of Amado ALONSO, stylistics may study a text both as *ergon* and as *energeia* (ALONSO 1942). Elsewhere (ENKVIST 1964) and in a somewhat different context I have suggested the terms STYLOLINGUISTICS or *SL* for the linguistic description of stylistically significant features, and STYLOBEHAVIOURISTICS or *SB* for attempts at correlating such stimuli with their responses. If we wish to venture into SB, we may frankly use ourselves as informants and try to verbalize and classify our responses and to correlate them with the stimuli that caused them. We may set up ideal responses such as those of RIFFA-TERRE's "Average Reader" (RIFFATERRE 1959), we may observe informant behaviour, and we may try to elicit descriptions of responses from informants or informant groups. The wells of literary criticism may of course be tapped for a wealth of responses to classic literary texts.

In the strict sense, stylolinguistics is concerned with the linguistic description of stylistic stimuli, as well as with the methods by which such stylistic stimuli may be defined and identified. To what extent the linguist should be concerned with people's responses to stylistic stimuli depends on where he wishes to place the borders of his own discipline. Responses to stylistic stimuli are important clues to the meaning of such stimuli, and meaning is certainly a central concern of all study of language. And in foreign-language teaching, every teacher is compelled to concern himself with giving his pupils the proper patterns of response to stylistic features. Thus, however alien the study of stylobehaviouristics may seem to some linguists, it is all the same an area that many of us must be concerned with, and an area that all linguists will gnore at their own peril.

3

STYLE, *LANGUE* AND *PAROLE*,
COMPETENCE AND PERFORMANCE

3.1 STYLISTIC VARIATION IN LINGUISTIC THEORY

In addition to devising linguistic methods for the identification
and description of stylistic stimuli, stylolinguists must try
to define the place of style in linguistic theories. Let us
therefore look at some of the ways in which linguists have
tried to fit stylistic variation into their theories.

3.2 SAUSSURE: *LANGUE, PAROLE*

One of the major topics in the discussions around the theory
of stylolinguistics has been the question whether style should
be regarded as part of *langue* or of *parole* in the famous
SAUSSUREan dichotomy. The definition is best given in the
words of SAUSSURE's text, remembering that *langue* and *parole* together form the total of *langage*;

La langue existe dans la collectivité sous la forme d'une somme d'em-
preintes déposées dans chaque cerveau, a peu près comme un dictionnaire dont tous les exemplaires, identiques, seraient répartis entre
les individus [. . .] C'est donc quelque chose qui est dans chacun d'eux,
tout en étant commun a tous et placé en dehors de la volonté des
dépositaires [. . .] De quelle manière la parole est-elle présente dans
cette même collectivité? Elle est la somme de ce que les gens disent,
et elle comprend: a) des combinaisons individuelles, dépendant de la
volonté de ceux qui parlent, b) des actes de phonation également
volontaires, nécessaires pour l'exécution de ces combinaisons. Il n'y a
donc rien de collectif dans la parole; les manifestations en sont individuelles et momentanées [. . .] (SAUSSURE 1955: 38)

Such dichotomies cannot be ignored by those interested in linguistic variation. But students of style have not been unanimous in their attitudes to, and comments on, the SAUSSUREan dichotomy. There are at least four different ways in which theorists of style have reacted to the distinction between *langue* and *parole*. One solution is to find stylistic subsections under each of these two concepts. Another is to equate stylistics with the linguistics of *parole*. Yet another is to declare that though SAUSSURE's distinction is too valuable to throw away altogether, it needs supplementing if it is to be salvaged for stylolinguistic use. Finally, some scholars discard or ignore SAUSSURE's theory, implying that it is poorly suited for the theory and study of style.

Those who wish to maintain *langue* and *parole* might, then, identify stylistics with the study of *parole*. But such views (e.g. NAERT 1949) lead to difficulties, however well they may work in the analysis of single texts by one individual. Some of the difficulties are methodological. If *langue* is only observable as an abstraction from *parole*, and if styles are only observable as results of comparison between one sample of *parole* and another, how can these two samples be compared without recourse to *langue*? That is, each sample supposedly reflects the same, underlying *langue*, which directs them and makes them commensurable. And if *langue* must be drawn into such comparisons, then style must be related to *langue* and not only to *parole*. Also, if *parole* is defined as non-collective, individual, and momentaneous, it does not cover all of the language variants that we may wish to label as styles. This is true of non-individual, collective, group styles regulated not only by demands of a single, individual speech act but by the wider norms of groups or communities. Indeed there are important categories of texts such as laws, statutes, and certain types of scientific communication in which writers often take great pains to repress all traces of individualism from their expression. Thus, even if individual styles fit nicely under *parole*, group styles seem to contain the interindividual and normative element which places them under *langue*.

Presumably these are the reasons why some scholars have maintained that each of the two spheres has its own stylistics. It has been suggested (e.g. VINOGRADOV 1963b) that the stylistics of language operates on the paradigmatic level, assigning stylistic values to each grammatical rule and lexical item. The stylistics of speech operates on the syntagmatic level and shows how the stylistic system of language has been used to form the style of an individual text. Thus the stylistic potentialities of the paradigmatic system are eclectically used by those generating texts: they choose features from the paradigmatic system and put them into linear, syntagmatic strings.

Another solution is to divide styles into two categories: group styles belonging to *langue*, and individual styles belonging to *parole*. Lubomir DOLEŽEL is one of the Czech scholars who have emphasized the distinction between the style of a single utterance, and the style of a category or type of utterance (DOLEŽEL 1960). The former is close to SAUSSURE's *parole*, as it implies the capacity of an individual to order certain features in a single utterance. But to study this aspect of utterances, we shall need a special theory of discourse which is not the same as stylistics:

La différence entre la théorie de l'énonciation et la stylistique réside dans le fait que celle-la examine l'aspect général de l'énonciation et les lois générales de sa structure linguistique, tandis que celle-ci étudie l'aspect spécifique des énonciations et les lois spécifiques de la structure linguistique des énonciations et des types d'énonciations. (DOLEŽEL 1960: 196)

The type of stylistics devoted to categories, not to single texts, must define and group its corpora by individuals, epochs, functions, or genres, all of which can be studied synchronically as well as diachronically. Particularly important are the functional styles defined by "le but général du complexe normalisé des moyens linguistiques" (DOLEŽEL 1960: 197). Four such functional categories used by Czech scholars are conversation, publicity, science, and artistic communication. In such frames, artistic style becomes but another functional style, not a special language system opposed to that of non-artistic communication as suggested by those Russian formalists who maintained that artistic language (and, most notably, poetry) is language oriented towards itself.

A similar principle of divorcing individual styles from group styles appears in Josef VACHEK's *Dictionnaire de linguistique de l'École de Prague,* where a distinction is drawn between SPECIAL LANGUAGES and FUNCTIONAL STYLES:

La différence entre la langue spéciale et le style fonctionnel est la suivante: le style fonctionnel est déterminé par le but concret de toute manifestation linguistique; il s'agit de la fonction de la manifestation linguistique (c.-à.-d. de la 'parole'), tandis que la langue spéciale est déterminée par le but général de l'ensemble normalisé des moyens linguistiques, elle est la fonction de la 'langue'. (VACHEK 1966: 44)

This elegant placing of special languages under *langue* and of functional styles under *parole* brings with it some difficulties, however. It tends to separate descriptions of individualistic styles from those of impersonal styles, the type of communication where individuals struggle to escape from the norm from the type where communicants do their utmost to efface all traces of themselves. For some purposes the latter might justifiably be regarded as 'special languages' or group styles even if they have a *but concret* like 'functional styles'.

Problems of these kinds have led some scholars to posit supplements to SAUSSURE's dichotomy. One well-known attempt in this direction is that of Eugenio COSERIU. In his essay "Sistema, norma y habla" (COSERIU 1962) he has rehearsed the arguments agains the *langue/parole* distinction and illustrated the need for an additional, third level, labelled as *norm* or *usage*, as an intermediary between the two. Another suggestion towards supplementing SAUSSURE comes from Luigi ROSIELLO, who adds two levels, usage and norm, and places them between *langue* and *parole* (ROSIELLO 1965). The structure of language both acts on, and is acted on, by usage; usage is linked to norm by the forces of standardization. The norm has both a grammatical and a stylistic component, and these two components of the norm join both the collective and the individual elements of usage finally to determine *parole*. Some Prague linguists have also developed a three-level approach: between the concrete speech event and the abstract sentence pattern there intervenes an utterance level which includes features such as functional sentence perspective (DANEŠ 1964).

In stylostatistics, too, there have been efforts to supplement SAUSSURE. Gustav HERDAN repeatedly pointed out that statistics had proved the soundness of two of SAUSSURE's fundamental principles: the arbitrariness of the linguistic sign, which is revealed by the stability of phoneme distributions in different samples of language, and the linearity of the *signifiant*, which appears in the harmony between vocabulary connectivit and the theory of random partitions. Further, the relation between *langue* and *parole* has a statistical equivalent in the relation between the statistical universe and the sample. As SAUSSURE was so obviously right in matters such as these, his basic ideas ought to be salvaged. On such grounds, HERDAN argued for the use of SAUSSURE's third, often ignored, concept, *langage*, which could be reinterpreted statistically as

the total of samples *(parole)* that can be withdrawn from the statistical universe, represented by *la langue* plus probabilities. (HERDAN 1964: 74)

Langage thus becomes the level of stylistic norms. HERDAN's writings are, however, sometimes diffident at this very point:

Whether *le langage* ought to be regarded as something different from *la langue*, or whether it is preferable to regard *la langue* as already incorporating these probabilities, this is really more a matter of taste and definition, and I personally would not put much weight upon one in preference to the other conception. (HERDAN 1964: 74)

What is clear is that we need a level of norms incorporating not only structures but also their probabilities of occurrence — a point we shall return to, and one whose relevance has already appeared. If such a level can be incorporated into *langue*, well and good; if not, it must be given a zone of its own in linguistic theory. HERDAN was right in emphasizing that the existence of styles compels us to have, somewhere in our theory, a level with structures as well as their probabilities. It is not enough to have two levels only, one of structures without probabilities (*langue*) and another of features bound to a given text (*parole*).

In his studies of linguistic aspects of literary communication, Archibald A. HILL has also reminded us that SAUSSURE's two levels do not suffice. HILL's addition is a third element labelled as *interpretation* (HILL 1964). When hearing successive features of a text, says HILL, the receiver interprets them, apparently with the aid of projection rules which bring previous signals to bear on later ones and narrow down the range of possible interpretations. In the words of Professor HILL,

These successive interpretations are like hypotheses. They are not the same thing as *parole*, since they are conclusions about *parole*. They are not the same thing as *langue*, since if they were we should be forced to suppose that *langue* changes with each change in interpretation (HILL 1964: 44).

Interpretation is relevant to stylistics because style can be regarded as the aggregate of contextual probabilities. And this aggregate of probabilities is based on the receiver's past experience, which determines and guides his interpretation. If I have understood HILL correctly, his "interpretation" is closely related to HERDAN's *langage* and to the stock of norms and norm-conditioned expectations against which we match the texts we are exposed to.

In effect, HILL's interpretation, HERDAN's probabilities, and COSERIU's and ROSIELLO's levels of norm and usage all serve one basic requirement. They insert a probabilistic level between a more or less deterministic grammar, in which rules are given without the frequencies in which they are used in different contexts, and the taxonomic description of actual occurrences of grammatical features in a limited text. This is important in more than one respect. First it suggests that dichotomies such as the SAUSSUREan may not give an adequate base for linguistic theories that have expressly to cater for style. Secondly, in a wider connection it shows that the human element of linguistic experience must be reckoned with at some place of a complete theory of language. For, if probabilistic levels are necessary, and if our sense of linguistic probabilities is determined by our past experience of language, this past experience becomes a very major force in shaping our ability to generate and to interpret linguistic texts. We carry with us not only a deterministic, all-or-nothing grammar, but also a body of statistical data which we extrapolate from past experience into current probabilities and expectations.

3.3 CHOMSKY: *COMPETENCE, PERFORMANCE*

In transformational grammar, the counterpart of the SAUSSUREan dichotomy is the distinction between competence and performance. To cite a paper by Noam CHOMSKY from the mid-sixties:

A distinction must be made between what the speaker of a language knows implicitly (what we may call his *competence*) and what he does (his *performance*). A grammar, in the traditional view, is an account of competence. It describes and attempts to account for the ability

of a speaker to understand an arbitrary sentence of his language and
to produce an appropriate sentence on a given occasion. (CHOMSKY
1966: 3)

I take it this statement, and other similar ones, were not
composed especially to cater to theories of style, which
were not a focus of interest in early transformational grammar. In fact the notion of performance has more often been
evoked to explain those deviations from grammaticality that
are characteristic of ordinary speech. Nor should we here
spend much time in trying to analyse the precise differences
between competence and SAUSSURE's *langue*. It must suffice
to note that CHOMSKY's wordings suggest a greater emphasis
on an individual's internalized set of language rules, whereas
SAUSSURE brought in the social, interindividual aspect as
basic for *langue* (LEVIN 1965). Therefore it may be easier to
build an individual's past experience into competence than
into *langue*.

We might, however, ask, where should styles go, into
competence or into performance? If a person knows implicitly
that a text he hears or reads is in, say, legal style, and if he is
also capable of generating texts in this style, then one might
argue that the characteristics of legal style should be regarded as part of his competence. If so, a full analysis of competence should include an apparatus describing stylistic
variation. And if grammar must be capable of accounting for
a speaker's ability to understand an arbitrary sentence, and
if understanding the impact of the style of an arbitrary
sentence is part of this ability, it follows that a full grammar
must be concerned with style as well. Indeed CHOMSKY's very
words "to produce an appropriate sentence on a given occasion" (CHOMSKY 1966: 3) echo the sentiments of generations
of normative rhetoricians and teachers of style, who have insisted that a sentence is not appropriate if it is not dressed in
the style proper for the occasion. In this light it is interesting
to recall once again that early transformational grammar was
but little concerned with style. In fact the term *stylistic*

variation was often used to indicate that such variation need not be exhaustively analysed within the basic grammar or even within competence, but could be relegated to some other, less fundamental part of linguistics, and perhaps to performance. Another difficulty was caused by the lack of interest in, and even hostility to, statistics in early transformational grammar. Historically, this is easy to explain as one of the reactions against behaviourist doctrine. But if styles remain intimately linked to frequencies, we must find some way of quantifying our generative-transformational rules if we wish to include a stylistic component in our accounts of linguistic competence.

In the description of texts, it is of course perfectly possible to analyse their grammatical characteristics and styles with the aid of a generative-transformational model. We may readily state how many times a given writer used a certain rule when producing a given text (assuming that we have an adequate transformational grammar at our disposal). And we can do this even though styles and quantifications were not built into the grammar itself. (This is the reason why style has been regarded as part of performance, not competence.) But if we agree that linguistic variation must be explained in the rules themselves, we might try to provide our rules with an additional apparatus of quantification. This need has been met by KLEIN (1965) and by LABOV in his study of the copula in American ghetto English (LABOV 1969). LABOV found that only a statistical apparatus could adequately describe the type of free variation that occurred in his materials. That is, some variation was found to remain "free" in spite of the search for new parameters which could have determined when each variant was used. LABOV was therefore dissatisfied with the traditional type of transformational grammar, in which every rule either operates or does not operate depending on the presence or absence of explicit, rule-activating features or feature combinations. He needed a grammar whose rules were activated in a certain percentage of the instances but which remained inactive in the rest. As LABOV's method is of potential interest also to students of style, precisely because it shows us an example of how probabilistic quantification can be built into a generative grammar, it should be briefly presented here.

LABOV starts out by noting that current rules in generative grammar have the general form $X \to Y/A - B$. That is, every time X occurs in the environment $A - B$, it is rewritten as Y; otherwise the rule does not operate. Such rules are CATEGORICAL INSTRUCTIONS. If we introduce OPTIONAL RULES into our grammar, as CHOMSKY had done in his original 1957 format, we sidestep the crucial question as to when a rule is actually used and when it is not. Therefore the solution is to introduce VARIABLE RULES with a

specific quantity φ which denotes the proportion of cases in which the rule applies as part of the rule structure itself. This proportion is the ratio of cases in which the rule actually does apply to the total population of utterances in which the rule can possibly apply, as defined by the specified environment, if it were a categorical rule [. . .] (LABOV 1969: 738)

The values for φ range from 0 to 1. For categorical rules, the value for φ is always 1, and the rule always operates if triggered off by the environment.

It becomes convenient to define $\varphi = 1 - k_0$, where k_0 is the VARIABLE INPUT TO THE RULE which limits its application. The greater the value of k_0, the more rarely the rule operates. If we need a more elaborate formula to compute φ not in terms of a single factor but in terms of several variables, we may use

$$\varphi = 1 - (k_0 - \alpha k_1 - \beta k_2 \ldots - v k_n) \,,$$

where $k_0 \ldots k_n$ are empirically determinable constants, and $\alpha - v$ their weights. Here the formula was designed so that the presence of a positive constant in a given subset of sentences will diminish k_0 and thus increase the application of the rule by decreasing constraints and increasing φ. In principle one might think in terms also of negative constants or constraints, and write another formula with pluses instead of minuses within the parentheses.

When the values of the various constants have been determined through empirical study of the data, they may be arranged into a single hierarchy. The criterion for this ordering is that each constraint should outweigh the effects of all constraints below it in the hierarchy. This ordering helps us to put related constraints into a single system and thus to get a more accurate idea of their connections. Hierarchization is therefore an improvement over putting each constraint into a separate rule. It will also help to spot those constraints that fail to fit into the system and that will need rules of their own.

3.4 WAYS OF DESCRIBING STYLES WITHIN GRAMMAR

The dichotomies betwen *langue* and *parole* or between competence and performance serve to reconcile two views: language as a rule-bound system, and language as a wide range of behaviour. As the study of linguistic variation goes on, the discovery of new regularities may warrant moving certain areas of language from *parole* into *langue*.

Assuming that we have opted for describing stylistic variation in grammar proper, and not in *parole* or performance or some other extragrammatical limbo, how should we proceed? Obviously, we must mark our rules for stylistic applicability. Some types of stylogrammatical rules are categorical within each style. Thus we may wish to generate a religious text which always uses *thou lovest*, never *you love*. Other stylogrammatical rules are variable in LABOV's sense. We might, for instance, conceive of a scientific style in which the passive transformation operates in a given percentage of all sentences with certain specified underlying subjects (such as *I, we, the author(s) of the present paper*, etc.). We shall therefore need two kinds of stylogrammatical rules, categorical and variable, in addition to a battery of marks explaining the contextual range of application of each rule.

But there are some other basic decisions that have to be made first. One decision concerns the attribution of a given text to a given language. Should, say, Shakespeare's style, the style of Dr Johnson, and the style of Dylan Thomas all be regarded as subvarieties of one single language, English, or should they be regarded as separate languages meriting grammars of their own? Such decisions are made on cultural and widely sociolinguistic, not on grammatical, grounds. There is no linguistic definition of 'language' and 'dialect' that agrees with the traditional use of such terms. For instance, there are dialects traditionally labelled as "Norwegian" that are more readily intelligible to speakers of some Swedish dialects than to speakers of some other "Norwegian" dialects. Nevertheless such decisions are important. If we decide that Shakespeare, Dr Johnson, and Dylan Thomas all wrote the same language, though in different styles, we must design our description of that language to incorporate descriptions of these three styles within the same general frame. If not, we are free to describe each style in its own terms, without glancing — or "squinting", as linguists once used to say — at the others.

In this particular instance, the answer may seem obvious enough. If we write separate grammars for Shakespeare, Dr Johnson, and Dylan Thomas, we lose a lot in economy, because a very large number of statements will have to be repeated in each grammar. Also we run the risk of making the three grammars incommensurable. We may design them so differently that their comparison becomes awkward and laborious, though we know that such comparison is motivated by the fact that a vast number of people agree in calling them part of one and the same language, English. There was, however, a period when linguists used to insist that each text had to be described exclusively in terms of its own, immanent categories that were actually and overtly manifested on the surface of that text. Importing categories from other texts — not to speak of categories from other languages — was forbidden. Absurdly rigid adherence to such principles would, of course, make stylistic analysis difficult or even impossible. To guarantee easy comparison, texts that are commonly and justifiably regarded as part of the same language should be described within the same basic grammatical frame.

Once we have decided that there is sufficient cultural justification for regarding a set of texts as being in the same language, we must decide how the description of that language is to incorporate the description of its variants. We may scatter stylistic information throughout the grammar, explaining stylistic variation in connection with each rule. Rules would then contain a contextual matrix showing in what constellations of contextual features they operate, and how often (categorically and always, or with what probability). Or we may write a basic, stylistically neutral grammar incorporating only those features that appear in all styles — a grammar of the *degré zero* — and then add a set of sections that explain how the stylistically unmarked language described in the basic part of the grammar can be further developed into stylistically marked language. The former method harmonizes with the view that every text has a style and that there is no styleless or prestylistic expression. The latter assumes that there is a stylistically unmarked core out of which stylistically marked texts can be generated through the addition, subtraction, or transformation of certain specifiable features.

In theory, both methods have advantages and disadvantages. Writing a "neutral" grammar with stylistic appendices would most probably be the more difficult of the two approaches. Granted, methods such as factor analysis and numerical taxonomy (KRAUS – POLÁK 1967, CARVELL – SVARTVIK 1969) might be used as aids to reveal the structures that are shared by a sufficient number of texts to qualify as stylistically unmarked and neutral in the statistical sense. But the assignation of stylistically marked or unmarked status to grammatical features is likely to involve more than mere statistical weights. If such a grammar could be written, it would, however, be of considerable interest. It would also have practical applications for instance in foreign-language teaching, for it would focus attention on the contextually most neutral, most widespread, and in this sense basic, features of the language.

All the same there are strong reasons for agreeing with David CRYSTAL and Derek DAVY, who prefer to scatter stylistic information into the grammar. This, they say,

has the advantage of allowing easy comparative statement [. . .] Thus when the grammar defines the notion of sentence, all stylistically interesting points about sentence-types, distribution, *etc.* are described; when the grammar goes on to discuss adjectives in nominal groups, all significant stylistic points about adjectives are described, and so on. Such an approach means that in order to obtain a complete description of any one variety a description has to be pieced together by working through the grammar in some predetermined way, and noting points about a variety as they arise; but this is no objection to the approach, as it would in any case be necessary to work through the grammar in this way in order to specify the common-core information. (CRYSTAL—DAVY 1969: 42–3)

CRYSTAL and DAVY were working with practical goals in mind. Their worry is not only theory but also the convenience with which the user of a grammar may extract its stylistic information.

3.5 CHOICE OF DELICACY LEVELS

One of the remaining problems is ubiquitous. It concerns the choice of the optimal LEVEL OF ABSTRACTION for description of styles, or, to use M. A. K. HALLIDAY's excellent term, the choice of DELICACY LEVELS. In practice, if we write a grammar of a language, we must decide not only how and where we are going to put stylistic information, but also how much of such information we should be concerned with. Should we describe a few of the most important, major stylistic categories, or should we aim at greater delicacy and try to describe a large number of styles? We should note that if style is regarded as the result of density comparisons between text and norm, the number of possible styles is unlimited and depends on the number of possible combinations of texts and norms. In this sense, all 'styles' cannot possibly be described within one grammar, and the investigator is bound to decide where lies the point of diminishing returns for his particular purpose.

3.6 STYLISTIC RULES

Finally, what should our rules look like? Their form will of course depend on what model we choose for our grammar. Some requirements are, however, general enough to apply to all grammars, and they were already touched upon above. Thus, if a grammar is to cater for stylistic variation, con-textual matrices and indications of rule applicability in each constellation of contextual features must accompany each rule to mark its stylistic applicability and thus its stylistic value. More will be said about such requirements below in section *5.2.*

CONTEXT PARAMETERS

4.1 NEED FOR CONTEXT CLASSIFICATION

In the previous chapter I tried to list some general problems concerning the ways in which descriptions of styles could be fitted into linguistic description and into grammar. One of the statements most frequently emphasized in the course of the argument so far has been the role of contexts as determinants of styles. Indeed styles have been defined as those variants of language that correlate with contexts. Before going on I should therefore discuss some questions of the classification of contexts as a background for the definition and determination of styles.

If style is defined as contextually restricted linguistic variation, stylolinguistics must be capable of defining contextual ranges and restrictions. Many linguists have in fact tried to ignore, or even hedge, this task. To set up classifications and taxonomies for all the situations in which language may occur is admittedly a difficult operation. It has been doubly uncongenial to those linguists who are used to strict limitations of their subject and to such stringent methods as are possible if one works with narrow problems. Indeed there are linguists who confess defeat when facing the need for bringing taxonomic law and order into the welter of situations and contexts offered by the world's endlessly varied sociophysical settings. Still, linguistics has on the whole succeeded well in extracting relevant features out of very complex chains of events. For instance, phonologists have not been entirely defeated by the great complexity of the acoustic speech stream: their efforts

to distinguish between distinctive and redundant features have
yielded fairly good results. And the classification of linguistic
contexts is still likely to be simpler than the classification of
chains of events in, say, history or even the history of art.
However awkward context classification may be, there is no
way around it. We can neither ignore the fact that language
occurs in speech situations, nor can we wait for non-linguists
to present context taxonomies tailored expressly for stylolinguistic use. A full study of language must recognize the fact
that linguistic systems are used by living people in complex
environments.

4.2 RELATIONSHIPS OF CONTEXT AND LANGUAGE

Connections between variants of language and contexts can
be established in two ways. One of the approaches is from contextual categories: we may start out from a contextually definable body of text and see what types of language occur
within this corpus. We may thus study the language of an
individual, of a genre such as scientific communication, of a
period such as the eighteenth century, and so on, and compare
this language with that of a relevant norm to pinpoint its
own distinctive characteristics. But we may also approach
the problem in reverse and study the contextual spread of
certain linguistic features. We might, for instance, go through
a corpus of contemporary English texts looking for the forms
thou lovest and *he loveth,* and define all the passages dominated
by these forms as 'archaic'. In practice, all of us use both
methods. When we are exposed to texts in context, we norm-
ally start from the contexts and learn what linguistic features
tend to occur in them. When we see a text without a context
— say, the first paragraph of an unknown typescript without
a headline — we apply our knowledge in reverse and conjure
forth a probable context to fit the language. Once we can
establish firm connections between a certain range of contexts

and a linguistic form (for instance between *thou lovest* and Biblical or archaic style), we may use this linguistic form *(thou lovest)* as a criterion for context classification, and label every context in which it occurs with the proper label. In some instances, such a procedure works very well. In others, where the style markers are more complex and styles more varied and open-ended, firm connections are harder to establish. Still, in principle it is possible to proceed in both directions: to define sets of linguistic forms with the aid of the contexts in which they occur, or to define contexts with the aid of the linguistic forms that occur in them.

In cultures with stable relationships between context and language, such correlations are firm and therefore comparatively easy to establish. Historians of stylistics have duly noted that fixed correlations between genre — that is, traditional literary context — and style go back a long way. In book III, chapter xii of the *Rhetoric*, ARISTOTLE noted that each kind of rhetoric has its own appropriate style, and that the styles of speech and writing are different. The text usually given pride of place in histories of stylistics is, however, the *Rhetorica ad Herennium*, which had this to say about genre and style:

Sunt igitur tria genera, quae genera nos figuras appellamus, in quibus omnis oratio non vitiosa consumitur: unam gravem, alteram mediocrem, tertiam extenuatam vocamus. Gravis est quae constat ex verborum gravium levi et ornata constructione. Mediocris est quae constat ex humiliore neque tamen ex infima et pervulgatissima verborum dignitate. Adtenuata est quae demissa est usque ad usitatissimam puri consuetudinem sermonis. (CAPLAN 1954: 252)

The grave style, says the author, expresses ideas through the most ornate words, and should be used in the discussion of serious and grave matters. It is illustrated by a grand speech before a jury. The middle style is illustrated by a more relaxed speech for a jury, and the low style with a colloquial passage on an incident at the baths. Out of such beginnings grew the rigid theory of levels of style, which worked excellently as long as literature was closely tied to the corresponding genre categories (QUADLBAUER 1962). But when borders between genres became diffuse, the distinction between their styles was blurred, too. We may conclude that there tends to be a connection between the fixity of genres and the fixity of styles: a stable inventory of contexts suggests a stable inventory of styles. A society with very complex context parameters and context constellations could be expected to have very complex sets of styles as well.

4.3 APPROACHES TO, AND TAXONOMIES OF, CONTEXT

Contexts have been variously defined by different scholars. An example of a very inclusive definition is that of SLAMA-CAZACU (1961: 209): here context is a function of the INTENTION of the communication, the MEANING of the text, and the recipient's possibilities of INTERPRETATION. RIFFATERRE (1960) distinguishes between a MICROCONTEXT, which forms the stylistically unmarked set of constituents against which a stylistic device stands in contrast, and a MACROCONTEXT or that part of the message which precedes the stylistic device and is exterior to it. He has also defined context as "a linguistic pattern suddenly broken by an element which was unpredictable" (RIFFATERRE 1959: 171). RIFFATERRE's context thus emphasizes the role of the textual environment, whereas SLAMA-CAZACU brought in a number of factors from beyond the text.

Once again, we should admit that the range and detail of contextual features we should reckon with are determined by our problem and by our materials. In classifying contexts, the first task is to decide what features in them are STYLISTICALLY RELEVANT and what features are STYLISTICALLY IRRELEVANT or REDUNDANT. As this distinction may be of great importance, in some types of work it may be wise to use different terms for the total, "etic" textual and situational environment, and for our "emic" selection of stylistically significant features from among the endlessly large number of characteristics of a given sociophysical setting. One could, for instance, use the term ENVELOPE for the totality of features, and the term CONTEXT for the aggregate of stylistically significant features.

Every situation contains an infinite number of constituent features. The totality of such features, which also includes the time and place of the communication act, will in practice make the sociophysical envelope of every text unique. Precisely as in phonemic or distinctive-feature analysis of the speech stream, or in the kinesic analysis of gesture (BIRDWHISTELL 1952, SEBEOK 1964), our task is to extract the significant contexts from among the welter of features in the envelope. In other words, we should find the proper level of abstraction and of delicacy. And the method is, in principle, precisely the same as in phonemics or kinesics: we must isolate those recurrent features that prove to have an invariant relation to specific linguistic features. We must, in other words, eliminate redundant features that have no stylistic significance. When stated thus, the problem of context analysis should at once look more familiar and less forbidding. Nor should this approach be taken to suggest that all redundant features are necessarily meaningless. In phonology, allophonic and paralinguistic features also have meanings at certain levels: they may help us to identify speakers by voice colour or idiolectal mannerisms, and so forth. Similarly, stylistically redundant features of the sociophysical envelope may be of great interest in many ways, though we may decide to call them redundant in our quest for parameters of style.

We should, then, try to isolate those features from the sociophysical envelope whose presence or absence correlates with the frequency, presence, or absence of specific linguistic features. Let us take an example. John Smith is writing. He is in fact typing in his study at midnight. It rains. Now the rain may be irrelevant to this choice of language: we are not likely to find that Smith's expression will change with every squall.

The fact that he is writing at midnight may be relevant at a very delicate level of analysis: he may be tired, he may express himself less tersely and grammatically than he does when he is fresh in the morning, he may be less able to avoid undesirable individual idiosyncrasies. His typing might also affect his language: had he dictated the text, his sentences might have been more complex and rambling and contained more embeddings, as happened to Henry James. Such features are relevant at a very delicate level of analysis; yet such delicate analyses may be called for in certain studies of literary style. All the same, John Smith's choice of language is much more likely to be decisively affected by the purpose and recipient of the text he is composing. It will make a great deal of difference whether he is writing a love letter, a letter to the Editor of *The Times*, a legal brief, or a note for his son who has overspent his allowance. And the very fact that he is writing will also have a profound effect on his language: he would put things differently were he speaking on the telephone.

One reason why it would be overambitious to begin by attempting inventories of contextual universals is that a taxonomy of contextual features is closely bound to each culture and to each sociolinguistic situation. The contextual spectrum of Eskimo is different from that of Yoruba, and both differ from that of English. Japanese is often cited for its complicated and subtle systems of *keigo* or 'honorific language', whose distinctions readily strike Europeans as complicated. Its various inflexional forms must be analysed in terms of three-dimensional, or perhaps even multidimensional, system, two of whose axes are the axis of attitudes to the conversation partner (plain to polite) and the axis of attitudes to the subject matter (humble to exalted). To translate *keigo* styles into European languages is far from easy. At a level of greater delicacy, even the languages of Europe will be found to have different contextual spectra. It is therefore wise to start by assuming that contextual taxonomies are culturally restricted rather than universal. This also suggests that the categories of style of one language do not necessarily have exact equivalents in another language, and raises a host of questions related, among other things, to the theory of translation.

In the extraction of stylistically significant contextual features from the sociophysical envelope we shall, however, need a conceptual frame and a terminology. And once this frame can be made universal, general, and inclusive, the features actually used in individual languages and styles can be regarded as selections from it. So far, different scholars have arrived at very different terminologies, though sometimes their terminologies disguise considerable similarities of thought. For instance, I have here used the short and therefore convenient term CONTEXT as a blanket both for the textual and for the situational features in the envelope surrounding a given linguistic unit. Others prefer to make a clear-cut distinction between SITUATION and CONTEXT, reserving the latter for INTRATEXTUAL CONTEXT or CO-TEXT.

Some schools of linguists, including the Prague school and many Soviet scholars, have written about functional styles in a way which suggests that the "functions" in fact represent major constellations of contextual features. The difficulty with the term *functional style* has been that — even apart from its mathematical senses — the term *function* has been understood to mean very different things. First, one well-known set of linguistic functions is that defined by Roman JAKOBSON in his famous paper "Linguistics and poetics" (JAKOBSON 1960). Here JAKOBSON listed six factors: addresser, message, addressee, context, contact, and code, which are inalienably present in all verbal communication. Each factor has a corresponding function. Though each message is likely to fulfill more than one function at once, it is still characterized by a hierarchic ordering of the six functions. Thus each text is dominated by one of six universal functions: the COGNITIVE or denotative or referential function related to context; the EMOTIVE function focussed on the addresser; the CONATIVE function oriented towards the addressee; the PHATIC function with emphasis on contact; the METALINGUISTIC function centred upon the code; and the POETIC function linked with the message itself. Secondly, other adherents of the term *functional style* have equated their functions, not with JAKOBSON's universals but with culturally conditioned, significant contextual groupings very much akin to genres. Among functional styles they list the styles of scientific, journalistic, artistic, poetic, colloquial, and perhaps other types of communication. Thirdly, the meaning of the term *function* has been diluted by yet another sense perhaps best describable as "functional efficacy": a style is functional if it works efficiently in a given situation.

In another book (ENKVIST – SPENCER – GREGORY 1964) I tried to set up a relatively weakly ordered list of the contextual features that may deserve consideration in stylistic analysis and from among which the significant features could be extracted. The inventory looked as follows:

textual context
    linguistic frame
        phonetic context (voice quality, speech rate, etc.)
        phonemic context
        morphemic context *(he sings / he singeth)*
        syntactic context (including sentence length and complexity)
        lexical context
        punctuation, capitalization
    compositional frame
        beginning, middle, or end of utterance, paragraph, poem, play, etc.
        relationship of text to surrounding textual portions
        metre, literary form, typographical arrangement
extratextual context
    period
    type of speech, literary genre, subject matter
    speaker/writer

listener/reader
relationship between speaker/writer and listener/reader in
    terms of sex, age, familiarity, education, social class
    and status, common stock of experience, etc.
context of situation and environment
gesture, physical action
dialect and language

I further noted that if items from this list are regarded as
stylistic characteristics, they must be omitted from the context and transferred to the category of potential style markers.

Such unordered lists are, however, merely a starting-point
for context taxonomies. In British linguistics, for instance,
some significant contributions have appeared in the past
several years. SPENCER and GREGORY are among those who
have emphasized the need for "placing" a text, first into its
proper historical and dialectal setting, and then by three contextual parameters called FIELD, MODE, and TENOR of discourse
(ENKVIST – SPENCER – GREGORY 1964: 85–91). FIELD re-
lates the discourse to its subject matter. Thus for instance an
article on nuclear physics and a love letter differ in field. In
long texts, the field may shift: in novels, for instance, a
novelist is likely to move from one field to another. By MODE,
SPENCER and GREGORY mean

the dimension which accounts for the linguistic differences which
result from the distinction between spoken and written discourse.

They carefully note that in some texts such as poems, authors
may be very conscious of the spoken mode though they are in
fact writing, and that the devices used by novelists and
dramatists to provide an illusion of natural speech are part of
the modal dimension. The difference between scripted and unscripted speech should also be noted here. The third parameter,
TENOR, reflects the relationship between the speaker/writer
and the listener/reader, chiefly in terms of degrees of formality
on a continuous scale between extreme formality and extreme

informality. These five dimensions — period, dialect, field, mode, and tenor — of course also interact. For instance, field is likely to affect tenor. An article on physics is likely to use more formal tenors than a love-letter.

In their discussion of dimensions of situational constraint, CRYSTAL and DAVY attempted a further refinement of similar variables. Their system looks like this (CRYSTAL — DAVY 1969: 66):

A. Individuality
   Dialect
   Time
B. Discourse
   (a) [Simple/Complex] medium (speech, writing)
   (b) [Simple/Complex] participation (monologue, dia-
       logue)
C. Province
   Status
   Modality
   Singularity

The features under A and B should explain themselves. Under C, PROVINCE reflects occupational or professional activity: the languages of public worship, advertising, science, or law each have their own province. STATUS is the term for the relative social standing of the communicants in terms of formality, respect, politeness, intimacy, kinship, business relations, and the like. MODALITY covers differences in the form and medium of communication such as those between a letter postcard, note, telegram, memo, lecture, report, essay, monograph, or textbook. SINGULARITY is a term for occasional, personal idiosyncrasies which are said to differ from those under "individuality" in that

the former are typically short, temporary, and manipulable, usually being deliberately introduced into a situation to make a specific linguistic contrast, whereas the latter are relatively continuous, permanent, and not able to be manipulated in this way — in short, non-linguistic. (CRYSTAL – DAVY 1969: 76)

To mention yet another attempt at an inventory of context parameters: in a paper on the linguistic theory underlying the teaching of Russian to foreigners, VINOGRADOV and KOSTO-MAROV abandoned the usual inventory of functional styles and set up a system of five, mainly binary, categories (VINO-GRADOV – KOSTOMAROV 1967). They consisted of (1) means of communication: speech, writing, gesture, (2) presence *versus* absence of partner, (3) one-way or two-way flow of informa-tion, (4) individual *versus* mass communication, and (5) communication in contact or at a distance. With five binary features we get a theoretical number of $2^5 = 32$ possible com-binations.

An area in need of further research is the ordering and hierarchization of context parameters. For the rough group-ings in examples such as the above should not be taken to imply hierarchic ordering. As CRYSTAL and DAVY have emphasized, certain patterns of co-occurrence, and thus of redundancy, can readily be found. Legal language is usually formal, conversational language is probably informal, and legal language is very improbably ever colloquial. Observa-tions of this kind suggest that a certain amount of hierarchi-zation might be extracted out of large empirical materials on the co-occurrence of contextual parameters, and that certain redundancy rules could be set up to indicate for instance that the feature [+ legal] makes the feature [+ formal] unneces-sary to repeat. Still, we shall be likely to find that studies of context hierarchies will first of all necessitate a very sophisti-cated set of definitions of the parameters (thus two lawyers talking shop over a cup of coffee should not be said to use legal language if legal language is to be formal, not colloquial). And we may also find a large amount of overlap and fluctua-tion, less in cultures with stable context categories and more in societies with complex and fluctuating contexts and in situations where individual idiosyncrasies are permitted or even encouraged.

Some schools of linguists like to illustrate hierarchies with numbered brackets or tree diagrams, and sets of unordered features with matrices. The overlaps of stylistic categories seem to be easier to handle in matrices than in trees.

4.4 LINGUISTIC DIVISION OF TEXT INTO PORTIONS

It was noted above that the student of style is often able to start out by comparing a well-defined text with a well-defined norm. If so, his task is to find the linguistic features that make the text significantly different from the norm. But in some situations it is necessary to reverse the process, to start out from an undivided and massive body of text, and to see whether it can be divided into different portions by analysing the distribution of its linguistic features. If these linguistically distinct portions prove to correlate with contextual categories, their languages qualify as styles. Such investigations will profit from operations such as factor analysis (KRAUS – POLÁK 1967) and numerical taxonomy (CARVELL – SVARTVIK 1969). A representative example of this approach is a paper by A. JA. ŠAJKEVIČ. He asked the basic question, What allows us actually to classify a given variant of language as a style? Is there an objective method for distinguishing styles that makes it possible for us to assert that in a given body of text (or, why not, in an entire language) there are, say, five rather than six or ten or twenty "functional" styles? He then went on to analyse a corpus of one million words out of 307 texts by Elizabethan and early Stuart authors: 161 texts from plays (about half the corpus), 76 poetic texts (about one-fifth of the corpus), the Bible (8 per cent), prose fiction by Lyly and Deloney (5 texts; 4.5 per cent), Bacon (6 per cent), travel descriptions (4 per cent), letters, Royal edicts, and so on. By factor analysis by computer of the patterns of noun

modification, ŠAJKEVIČ obtained four major style categories:
a poetic group, a colloquial group, a factual group, and a religious or archaic group. The proportion of style markers
characteristic of each category could also be used to measure
the poetic, colloquial, factual, and archaic ingredients in
texts of any of the four major categories. This result was obtained through purely statistical methods, and it may be
said to correlate well with rough-and-ready intuitive catego-
rizations of Elizabethan and Early Stuart prose (ŠAJKEVIČ
1968). It would, however, be interesting to know whether
criteria other than noun modification might have suggested a
different taxonomy of major styles. Another example of a
somewhat similar approach, though with less emphasis on
formal statistics, is the study of Plato's styles by Holger
THESLEFF. By using close to one hundred grammatical and
rhetorical style markers and by studying the distribution of
a few hundred words, THESLEFF (1967) arrived at ten classes
or shades of style, as he called them. All of Plato's dialogues
contained more than one style, and some correlations could
be suggested between each style and contextual categories
such as speeches, myths, visions, mimetic play, parody, and
the like.

It might be added in passing that the identification of contexts by their style markers is by no means merely an exercise
for linguists or stylostatisticians. On the contrary, it charac-
terizes many types of communication. When A speaks to B,
B will readily draw conclusions from A's classification of the
context: he will, for instance, note what level of formality
and politeness A regards suitable for speaking with him. And
this leads to a mirror effect: B's ideas of A's ideas of B will
affect B's views of A, and also influence B's classification of
the context and hence his style.

There are thus occasions where contexts can be consciously
defined and even manipulated through choices of style, which
may range on a scale between extreme flattery and extreme
rudeness. The relation between context and style thus works

both ways: the use of language may influence context, and not only *vice versa*. A simple example. In Swedish, the reciprocal use of the familiar pronoun *du* has come to mark not only familiarity but also contexts in which the communicants wish to appear equal to emphasize in-group solidarity. From use between members of the same profession, *du* has now spread to more heterogeneous groups such as those working in universities and in large offices. There are instances in which heads of organizations have decreed the use of the familiar pronoun obligatory in all oral communication within the organization. That such decrees have been made indicates a belief in the power of style markers to define contexts: the universal use of a familiar pronoun within an organization presumably makes people happy because it marks contexts in which communicants have equal status. How long the effect of such reforms-by-decree will last is, unfortunately, another matter. If the use of, say, a familiar pronoun becomes universal, this pronoun will inevitably lose its power to function as a style marker and thus to identify contexts. In such instances, languages are likely to develop new means to mark those differences in context that a tacit consensus — or "usage" — finds in need of marking.

4.5 GROUP CONTEXTS. SLANG

This kind of linguistic dynamism in the realm of style leads us to the origin and formation of SLANG as well. Here, words play a decisive role as markers. Slang might be said to arise out of a given group's need to form a style of its own, again to mark solidarity within the group. If suitable markers for such an IN-GROUP STYLE do not already exist, they have to be created. The means are the same as in word formation. Old words can be used in new meanings and new contexts and collocations. New words arise through affixation. Loans can be brought in from other regional or social dialects, from neighbouring languages, and from other languages familiar to the group. Even root-creation may occur in slang. Particularly common are phonological neologisms such as abbreviations and clippings. In favourable situations, where the in-group is large and has a strong need for demonstrations of solidarity, the slang may spread very rapidly. But if a style-marker of slang is so successful that it passes into the language of other groups, or into general use, it loses its original function. Its originators may therefore have to adopt new slang terms. Another reason why slang may be ephemeral is that many groups are short-lived: more lasting groups tend to have more lasting slang.

SLANG is a relative term, not an absolute: the distinction between concepts such as 'slang', 'professional language', and 'sociolect' depends on our classification of groups of people (in-group, profession, social class) rather than on linguistic criteria. If a certain subvariety of language which was originally used by members of a restricted in-group when communicating within itself spreads to a whole social class, it stops being slang and becomes a sociolect. In turn, a sociolect may acquire more prestige than other sociolects and begin spreading, and even become a standard language. Once again, such considerations show the futility of setting up rigid borders between styles, slang, sociolects, and other linguistic diatypes. Among those who must closely follow the dynamics of these processes and keenly watch linguistic fashions are advertisers, especially those who appeal to groups such as teen-agers. Thus by the summer of 1970, former high-frequency expressions such as *jet set*, the adjective *swinging*, and *to be with it* were obsolescent in advertisements of charter-flight holidays for young British customers.

4.6 DYNAMISM IN CONTEXTUAL CATEGORIZATION

The lesson to be drawn from such considerations is that relations between contexts and styles must not be regarded as constant. In fact both the sociophysical envelope and the language used in a given contextual constellation are always subject to change. This means that the contextual probabilities of linguistic features are affected both by changes in contexts and by changes in language. All those interested in styles, whether linguists, literary scholars, advertisers, or others, should remember that in stylistics, too, strict synchrony and static views remain simplifications of a dynamic reality. Looking at styles as constants is a very useful working hypothesis which helps us to isolate features from their complex environment and thus to see them more clearly. But in stylistics, as in all linguistics, the complete view should be a panchronic synthesis of synchronic and diachronic considerations.

Special problems can also be caused by SHIFTS OF STYLE within a text. Some such shifts can be readily correlated with changes in context. In a novel, for instance, we are often able to distinguish between dialogue and non-dialogue, or between passages dominated by action and passages dominated by background description. Such contextually delimited portions of the text may have styles of their own. But sometimes writers and speakers achieve stylistic effects by changing their style without overt changes in context. It then becomes the reader's and listener's task to note that the relations between context and language have changed. Thus a writer may rise to a vigorously polemic climax after a calmly factual and deliberative passage. This may be reflected in an increase of certain syntactic features such as rhetorical questions and imperatives, and a higher incidence of evaluative or emotionally charged words. Another kind of example is available in Joyce's *Ulysses* in that famous passage where Joyce imitates a number of English literary styles from Old English to modern times. To grasp the effect of this passage, the reader must be capable of associating Joyce's variants of language with their proper diachronic contexts.

GRAMMATICAL MODELS
IN THE DESCRIPTION OF STYLE MARKERS

5.1 STYLE AS A DIFFERENTIAL

Though styles are varieties of language that correlate with specific constellations of contextual features, stylistic analysis must always be based on comparison, tacit or explicit. If we define a body of text by contextual criteria — say, a set of political leaders in *The Daily Mirror* — we can, of course, study its language and describe it in any manner we may wish. But such a description remains an account of the language, not the style, of this corpus. If we wish to spot those linguistic features that make political leaders in *The Daily Mirror* different from other kinds of texts — such as other types of articles in the same paper, political leaders in *The Times*, or any other texts that we define as relevant and sensible norms of comparison — we must match the densities of the linguistic features in our text against the densities of the corresponding features in the norm. Comparison is the only key to stylistic differentials, that is, to the style markers that characterize our text as different from other texts. And all stylistic descriptions must begin with an inventory of style markers.

This point has sometimes been obscured because so many students of style have operated with tacit rather than with explicit comparisons. Their norm has not been explicitly circumscribed and defined. It has remained a product of past experience of the uses of language in comparable contexts, and the comparison itself has been performed intuitively in the sense that some or all of the materials on which it was based are irrecoverable. Such tacit comparisons are very often expressed in impressionistic or metaphoric terms. An experienced reader may thus spot the style of a given text as "heavy". But he may not be able at once to describe what makes the text "heavy", whether the "heaviness" owes to a high density of difficult or long words, to long and complex sentences, to numerous embeddings, or to something else. A "heavy" text may also be "lighter" than many other texts, but still be "heavy" for its context: a sentence which strikes us as relatively short in a legal contract may appear very long on a postcard. As always, the norm, too, enters into the picture.

5.2 REQUIREMENTS FOR GRAMMATICAL MODELS

Such considerations help us to formulate the requirements that a model of language has to satisfy if it is to give us a good basis for stylolinguistic description. We might posit four basic requirements. First, the model has to allow for linguistic VARIATION and admit systematic description and classification of contextual categories. The second requirement demands CONSISTENCY: both text and norm have to be described in terms sufficiently similar and consistent to permit comparison. The third requirement has to do with ADEQUACY: the linguistic model chosen must be capable of describing all relevant style markers. The fourth requirement was dealt with in sections *3.2* and *3.3*: the model should admit both categorical and probabilistic rules.

We have already seen that linguists have made some beginnings towards the setting-up of taxonomic systems of context parameters. The purpose of such systems is to make possible the extraction of the stylistically significant contextual features out of the endlessly varied cultural and sociophysical envelope that surrounds language. Granted, the systems available today may well be characterized as sketchy, rough, and provisional. Still they are adequate for a number of practical tasks in the analysis and description of styles. These systems are not a prerogative of one or another linguistic movement or grammatical school. They may be used together with various grammatical models, though some models may well prove more hospitable to them than others.

The requirements of consistency and adequacy are even more directly relevant to the choice of linguistic models in the description of style markers and styles. Consistency can be dismissed briefly. As style is based on comparison, the descriptions of text and norm must be commensurable. Both must be described in terms sufficiently similar to allow comparison. I have already touched on this point above in section *3.4*. If the text and norm are described separately according to rigid principles of immanence, and if the two descriptions are to result in a maximally economic presentation of features overtly and manifestly present on the surface of the text and the norm, respectively, there is no guarantee that the two descriptions are fully consistent. Accidental differences of surface structure may lead to great differences in basic levels of the description, because certain structures did not happen to be overtly present in the text or in the norm. Text and norm, then, have to be described in sufficient depth and at optimal levels of abstraction and delicacy to allow for maximally meaningful comparison. Of course no levels of maximal meaningfulness can be set universally and *a priori*. For one task, one level is best; for another task, another level may be more rewarding.

The requirement of adequacy demands that the model be capable of describing all potential style markers. All linguistic features, as well as all combinations of linguistic features, in fact qualify as stylistic discriminators. In practice, however, we cannot sit back to wait for the ultimate perfection of grammar before we venture to describe styles. On the contrary, from the point of view of stylistics alone, any grammar that does the job is by definition adequate. This does not of course contradict the obvious fact that some grammatical models are more satisfactory than others. It only means that a number of style markers are linguistic features of a kind that can be described even with the aid of relatively simple, crude, and unsophisticated grammars. We do not, for instance, need particularly advanced grammars to study sentence length in written texts, numbers of finite verbs per sentence or per word, the ratio of adjectives per substantive (always assuming that our grammar gives exact, formal definitions of 'finite verb', 'sentence', 'adjective', 'substantive', and other such concepts), the density of passives, certain basic varieties of word-order patterns, and the like. Those who need an excuse for the crudeness of their grammatical apparatus may define their stylistics as a branch of applied linguistics, where the eclectic choice of simple approaches is a virtue and not a vice. On the other hand, those who analyse styles may not wish to stop at stylistic analysis. They may also wish to relate their findings to certain linguistic theories or to certain full descriptions of the language. If so, they should choose a model which makes this as easy as possible, even when this may complicate the definition of some individual style markers.

For some tasks, simple grammars will thus prove adequate. In other tasks, we may at once come up against the frontiers of current grammar and even of linguistics proper. If, for instance, the text and the norm are suspected to differ because one might have different metaphors from the other, we shall need a linguistic model capable of describing different types of metaphor. If the text seems to be characterized by a certain pattern of thematic progression, the grammar adopted must offer a system for the description of thematic movements from one sentence to the next. And what about irony? Experience tells us that a high density of ironical statements may well be a characteristic of a given style. But to what extent is irony — always including those irony signals which warn us to interpret a passage ironically rather than literally — definable by strictly linguistic methods? We should be duly encouraged by the fact that in recent years, linguistics has expanded rapidly and become increasingly concerned with problems of these kinds. Still, many features of great interest to students of style lie well beyond the current borders of rigorous linguistics. Meanwhile, work must go on. If the student of style cannot find what he needs in the linguistic models that are available, he has no choice but to look for help elsewhere, for instance in traditional rhetoric and semantics. And if this fails, he will have to devise concepts and methods of his own.

5.3 STYLE IN SOME GRAMMATICAL MODELS

Such liberal views have occasionally seemed vague, unscholarly, and therefore repugnant to those linguists who are dedicated to one grammatical model to the exclusion of all others. But even today, the world of grammar remains a pluralistic one. Linguists have not universally and unanimously agreed to regard any single grammatical model as superior to all others. On the contrary, several schools all speak for their own models. Even the much-reviled traditional grammar has been partially rehabilitated by some recent developments, though linguists are in reasonable agreement about its weaknesses and shortcomings. Tagmemic grammar is one of the major movements continuing the traditions of behaviourist structuralism, to which linguistics owes more than many tend to admit today. HJELMSLEVian glossematics has contributed not only valuable theoretical foundations but also some concrete descriptions of French and Danish. In Britain, the systemic grammar of M. A. K. HALLIDAY and others has gone through various stages of development in the past decade or so. Generative-transformational grammar has continued its triumphs ever since CHOMSKY's *Syntactic Structures* of 1957, but also given rise to new offshoots such as the deep-semantic transformationalism of LAKOFF, McCAWLEY, ROSS, and others, and the case grammar of FILLMORE.[1] It also has a

---

[1] See LAKOFF (1969), McCAWLEY (1968), ROSS (1970), FILLMORE (1969), and the readers BACH – HARMS (1968), FODOR – KATZ (1964), JACOBS – ROSENBAUM (1970), KIEFER (1969), and REIBEL – SCHANE (1969).

rival in LAMB's stratificational grammar. In the Soviet Union, ŠAUMJAN and his followers advocate their own variety of generative grammar which they call "the Applicational Model". To such lists, others might wish to add yet others of their favourite models of grammar.

It would take a library, not a book, to run through all these models, one after the other, and try to assess all of their relative advantages and disadvantages in solving a wide spectrum of different types of linguistic problems. All I wish to attempt here is a very brief discussion of a few points particularly relevant to stylistics.

In traditional grammar, the border towards rhetoric, and thus also towards stylistics, was left open. It was up to each grammarian to decide how much stylistics and rhetoric he wanted to put into his grammar. And, the other way round, rhetoricians were free to make what forays they liked into grammatical territory. This freedom was bought at the cost of weak systematization. Grammarians dealt with those features of a language that seemed important or interesting. They were at liberty to ignore the rest. Then, one of the common aims of traditional grammarians was to provide norms for writers and speakers. This, too, led to an intimacy between grammar and stylistics. In fact many of our traditional grammars, including a host of old school grammars, are treatises on style in so far as they mark certain structures as appropriate to certain occasions, and brand others as unsuitable (often in terms of 'right' and 'wrong').

Behaviourist-structuralist grammars were usually preoccupied with an objective description of the language actually occurring in a definite corpus. The corpus could consist of spoken or colloquial language, as in the grammars of Charles Carpenter FRIES. The restrictions placed on the corpus readily turned the grammars into descriptions of one style rather than into comparative analyses of whole ranges of different styles. Other circumstances contributed to the comparative neglect of stylistic considerations. Structuralists were anti-normative. They insisted on immanent descriptions, which did not encourage the comparison of different texts. And they were preoccupied with the surface of language, and even there with the smaller units such as phonemes and morphemes. This also led them away from style, which resides in the larger units as well as in the small ones.

Though the behaviourist-structuralist model was poorly adaptable to stylolinguistic description, this did not mean that its adherents wholly neglected stylistics. Though BLOOMFIELD himself avoided the word *style* in his classic *Language* (BLOOMFIELD 1933), many of his pupils and followers wrote about it. Bernard BLOCH elegantly and suggestively defined style as

the message carried by the frequency distributions and transition probabilities of its linguistic features, especially as they differ from those of the same features in language as a whole. (BLOCH 1953: 40)

In Zellig HARRIS's papers, including those on discourse analysis, keys to style are sought in distribution. (HARRIS 1952a, 1952b). Martin Joos's *Five Clocks* (JOOS 1962) contains a wealth of acute observations as well as an attempt to set up five major style categories for English: frozen, formal, consultative, casual, and intimate. Archibald A. HILL has written widely and incisively about ways of analysing literature with a linguistic apparatus, and also about the theoretical principles of stylistics. And Kenneth PIKE has been concerned with the place of language in a wider frame of patterns of human behaviour, which led him to set up concepts and categories useful to context analysts (PIKE 1967). But in spite of efforts such as these, it would be a distortion to say that the focus of behaviourist structuralism lay on stylolinguistics.

I have already noted that the early formats of transformational grammar were hardly more hospitable to style. Transformationalists tended to react against the behaviourists' preoccupation with the surface analysis of limited corpora, and this also prejudiced them against statistics. But I have also emphasized that we may count the rules and transformations that went into a given text, and that LABOV's variable-input rules in fact are an attempt to turn the originally categorical model into a probabilistic one better suited to the description of linguistic, including stylistic, variation. And transformationalists have yet other strings to their bow. For instance, they have helped to modify our attitudes to the problem of choice, which has bedevilled stylistics for a long time.

Style, many experts have maintained, arises as a result of CHOICE as a preference of one feature to another. However, there are other types of choice in language, in addition to stylistic choice. There is, first of all, PRAGMATIC CHOICE, which is based on the preference of one utterance to another because of its truth value. Thus a person may prefer to say *it is snowing*, not *it is raining*, because the former is true and the latter untrue (or the other way round, if he wants to mislead his hearers). Another type of linguistic choice is GRAMMATICAL CHOICE: English people prefer to say *he is here*, not *he am here* or *he are here*, choosing *is* because they wish to conform to the patterns of well-formed English. Neither of these types is identical with STYLISTIC CHOICE. Therefore those who wish to define style as the result of choice must also face the task of distinguishing stylistic choice from pragmatic and grammatical choice. This is far from easy. One criterion is given by the study of correlations: choices that correlate only with context are stylistic, whereas choices that correlate at least with expression content, and perhaps also with context, are pragmatic. As features with different expression content mean different things, this might be rephrased by saying that pragmatic choice takes place between features that have different meanings, whereas stylistic choice takes place between features which mean the same. "Mean the same", that is, apart from their stylistic meaning, which must still be regarded as part of the total meaning of an utterance. An example of stylistic choice would be the use of *he is a fine man* rather than *he is a nice chap*.

The view of style as choice has a lot to commend it. Among other things it agrees nicely with our intuition: we often feel how the choice of a certain word instead of another gives a definite stylistic texture and flavour to a sentence or passage. And when struggling for stylistic effect we often consciously seek *le mot juste* from among a set of words which all satisfy the pragmatic and grammatical requirements we wish to satisfy. There are two difficulties, however. First, with our present equipment it is hard to say which formal features — words or structures — mean sufficiently the same — or which correlations exist between formal features and their content — to qualify as stylistic, not pragmatic, variants. Our machinery of semantic analysis and description is rarely accurate and sensitive enough to provide us with firm information of this kind. In fact, the flow of information has so far been from stylistics and from the study of items in context to semantics rather than the other way round. Secondly, those grammatical models that dealt exclusively with the surface of a text were incapable of mapping out the processes of choice that underlay that surface. When the linguist saw the text, all choices had already been made. Choice, said the linguist, was beyond conjecture, and speculating about it was vacuous, rank mentalism.

If we ever have a model of language which allows us to chart all processes of choice and to list all the alternatives rejected and paths not taken, this objection will lose its main point. In principle, generative grammars ought to be capable of giving us a generative programme in which a large number of choices, except those of the deepest and most fundamental pragmatic meanings, are made explicit in the rules. It is another matter to say which type of generative grammar will best realize this formidable requirement. One might, for instance, indulge in speculations about deep semantic components generating prestylistic meanings, which form the input into a syntactic and lexical component sensitive to the textual and situational context of the utterance.

Deep meanings would then be marked with the appropriate matrix of constellations of stylistically relevant contextual features, which would either trigger off the generative processes characteristic of the appropriate style, or define a set of constraints preventing stylistically inappropriate transformations from taking place. If such inappropriate transformations actually do take place, the result will be a breach of style, a venture beyond the margin of tolerance. As I have noted before, style-sensitive rules may be of two kinds: some may be categorical and state that in a given style a given rule must operate either always or never, whereas others must be probabilistic and have a variable input which activates the rule in a certain percentage of the instances in which it could be activated.

In the light of such rather fanciful speculation it is interesting to note a nascent addition to the handling of some, though strictly limited, contextual features in transformational grammar. We owe this addition to John Ross. Briefly, in transformation grammar it has long been customary to regard certain constructions as results of deletion. An imperative such as *Go!* is thus a deletion of an underlying *You go*. Borrowing the concept of performatives from AUSTIN (1962), Ross turned these deletions into a system by positing the existence of a set of ABSTRACT PERFORMATIVE VERBS. Thus the sentence *Prices slumped* is a surface representation of an underlying structure with an abstract performative verb. (Cf. p. 77) If this abstract structure were to be verbalized as such, it would read something like *I tell you: prices slumped*. The performative superstructure *I tell you* is then deleted, and the output will be *Prices slumped*.

In his paper on declarative sentences Ross gives fourteen reasons in support of this particular brand of abstract syntax (Ross 1970). These reasons are not primarily stylistic in the sense of having been devised expressly to bring in features from the sociophysical envelope or from the stylistic context into grammar. They have to do with syntactic features such as the use of reflexive pronouns. Nevertheless it is clear that the performative superstructure refers to certain areas of situational context by referring to the speaker/writer, the listener/reader, and the "modality" of the sentence (its charac-

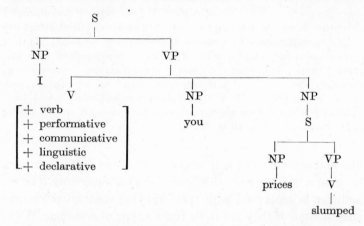

ter of statement, question, command, etc.). Ross's performatives might therefore be said to bring in some features of context into a deep layer of generative-transformational grammar. Ross himself has emphasized that one of the alternatives to PERFORMATIVE ANALYSIS would be PRAGMATIC ANALYSIS. In the latter, the underlying form of a sentence such as *Prices slumped* would be, simply, *Prices slumped*, plus — instead of the performative — a list of the contextual features present in the speech act. This list must have a form that is capable of triggering off or constraining syntactic processes. Its features must also be isomorphic with the system of performatives because they must be capable of doing everything performatives can do.

A precise [pragmatic] theory would have to specify formally what features of the infinite set of possible contexts can be of linguistic relevance. Furthermore, these features would have to be described with the same primes which are used for the description of syntactic elements, so that rules which range over syntactic elements will also range over them. While such a theory can be envisioned, and may even eventually prove to be necessary, it is obvious that it does not exist at present [...] If the pragmatic analysis is to be carried through, contexts must be assumed to have the structure of clauses: they must have elements which share properties with subject NP's, elements which share properties with indirect object NP's, and elements which share properties with verbs of saying. Furthermore, if Lakoff and I are correct in our claim that questions are to be derived from structures roughly paraphrasable by *I request of you that you tell me S*[...] then contexts also exhibit properties of syntactic constructions with embedded clauses. However, while such observations may be interesting, they only serve to illustrate the enormous gap between what can now be said about contexts in fairly precise terms and what would have to be said in any theory which could provide a detailed understanding of language use. (Ross 1970: 257-8)

The first sentence of the quotation will sound familiar enough to those who have read this book from the beginning. The remainder is concerned with the form that contextual features must assume if they are to fit Ross's type of grammar. Without minimizing the gap between syntax and stylistics one may still find it both interesting and promising that certain syntactic reasons have motivated the introduction of some contextual features into a deep component of syntax. Optimistic students of style might even be tempted to interpret performative analysis as another tiny step from grammatical theory towards stylistics. Certainly this type of inclusion of contextual features in a deep, possibly semantic component of generative grammar is more elegant and economical than a device which would, say, generate all possible stylistic variants of a given deep sentence, and then eliminate those that do not fit a given contextual matrix by straining the lot through a stylistic filter.

Transformational grammar has suggested further refinements that are potentially useful in the description of styles. We shall see in another chapter how it has modified our attitudes to deviant expressions. In the analysis of AMBIGUITIES, transformational grammar has suggested a clear theory: a given sentence is ambiguous *n* ways if it can be generated in *n* different ways. We should recall that at least since William Empson, ambiguities have been an important concern for students of literary styles. ELLIPSIS is another of the phenomena that can now be studied with more stringent methods than before. Structuralists could do little with ellipsis because they insisted that description be restricted to features actually present on the surface of the text: they failed to extend their use of the zero to the word level or above, though they used it freely in morphemics. And in the study of METAPHOR, which was one of the most recalcitrant problems of stylolinguistics, transformational grammar has also been beneficial. I shall return to this below.

5.4 TRANSFORMATIONAL GRAMMAR IN STYLISTICS

A pioneering attempt at using transformational grammar in the analysis of styles was that of Richard OHMANN (OHMANN 1964). He found certain uses of transformations characteristic of certain writers. His method was to go down to deeper structures from the surface of his texts by reversing the processes through which these texts had been generated. In the terminology of the early 'sixties, OHMANN was reconstructing the kernel sentences, and listing and counting the optional transformations between the kernel sentences and the textual surface. He found that Faulkner's apparent complexity was the result of surprisingly few — in fact mainly three — different transformations, all of which were additive in that they combined such kernel sentences as shared at least one morpheme. High frequencies of relativization, conjunction, and comparison were thus markers of Faulkner's style. The crucial features of a passage of Hemingway consisted of transformations that turn kernels into *style indirect libre* or *erlebte Rede*. In Henry James, the embedded elements outweighed the main sentence, and his style seemed to build on the positioning of structures rather than on the qualities of the

structures as such. D. H. Lawrence was OHMANN's example
of a writer whose style built largely on deletion. To repeat:
OHMANN had thus demonstrated the applicability of generative-transformational grammar to the description of styles,
irrespective of the fact that neither style nor frequencies had
occupied places of their own in transformational theory. The
patterns of frequency with which each writer had used certain
optional transformations and types of transformations proved
to be explicit, concretely describable style markers capable of
distinguishing between Faulkner, Hemingway, Henry James,
and D. H. Lawrence.

Since OHMANN wrote his paper, there have been several
other applications of transformational grammar to the description of styles (e.g. HAYES 1968). Also, as we have noted,
the transformational model has gone a long way since the late
'fifties and early 'sixties. Still the comparatively simple principles of the early format (CHOMSKY 1957), however unsatis-
factory they may seem in the light of later revisions, were quite
adequate for the analysis of a number of stylistic problems.
Distinctions such as those between kernels and transforms,
and between obligatory and optional transformations seemed
to harmonize nicely with some stylistic concepts and methods
of analysis. Thus a text could be reduced to its underlying
kernel sentences, which gave a reasonably well-defined
starting-point for descriptions of what a given speaker/writer
had done to produce the final text, even if one might hesitate
before equating the string of kernel sentences directly with
stylistically neutral or prestylistic expression. And the
contrast between obligatory and optional transformations
sounded familiar, and perhaps even congenial, to those who
liked to define style as choice from among the optional
features of language. Those students of style who wish to use
transformational models to describe a strictly limited range
of relatively simple syntactic structures may, in their practical
work, come to regret some of the later developments in transformational formats. They might even wish to return to

simpler models by omitting a number of such complications as are irrelevant to their particular problem. Here, too, the student of style may wish to feel free to use the simplest grammatical model that satisfies the requirements of his particular job.

5.5 SYSTEMIC GRAMMAR IN STYLISTICS

In recent British linguistics, the concern with style and register as well as with the linguistics of utterances has been more explicit, as one can expect of a school that acknowledges J. R. FIRTH as a major stimulus. I have already cited a number of examples of British discussions of contexts and context parameters, styles, and registers, and of fields, modes, and tenors of discourse. Some British achievements are particularly relevant to all students of stylistics. One is the theory developed by M. A. K. HALLIDAY and his collaborators. Here, languages are said to operate with four basic categories: unit, structure, class, and system. Units are arranged into structures, which are descriptions of syntagmatic strings. The category of class contains arrangements of units according to the way they operate. And the category of system is an inventory of those limited possibilities of choice that a speaker/writer has at a given place of the structure of language, the whole of a language being thus conceived of as a system of systems. HALLIDAY's model contains a number of other concepts vital to students of style as well, among them scale, cline, and delicacy. It is also strong on choice. In transformation grammar, all choices are usually built into a single system, which is split up into a very few components. In HALLIDAY's scale-and-category or systemic grammar, related choices are built into limited subsystems of their own. In practical application, this makes it easier to extract the subsystems one happens to need out of a systems model than out of a transformational model: one can use the relevant subsystem as an entity without having to involve oneself in more extensive and perhaps tenuous considerations. HALLIDAY's theory has also integrated certain essential areas of language that other models have found hard to include, among them transitivity and theme (HALLIDAY 1967–68). Its concepts have stimulated work in some fields that seem increasingly relevant to stylolinguistics, among them the cohesion of sentences in texts (HASAN 1968).

Another major feature of today's British linguistics is the rigorous processing of large masses of text. Professor Randolph QUIRK's Survey of English Usage at University College, London, has already resulted in a number of observations on usage that all students of English styles will find interesting. The methods of the Survey also contain relevant elements, among them the study of serial relationship which helps us to grasp the full complexities of linguistic subcategorization and gives us a means of contrasting actual occurrences with the range of theoretical choices. Problems of grammaticality and acceptability have been studied by means of elicitation experiments rather than through introspection (QUIRK – SVARTVIK 1966, GREENBAUM – QUIRK 1970), and the surveyors have also been concerned with prosodic and paralinguistic features in spoken texts (CRYSTAL – QUIRK 1964). These studies are worth the attention of all who investigate styles of English, partly because of the light they throw directly on subvarieties of English and their use, and partly because they offer concepts and methods that might be found suggestive in the analysis and description of styles.

5.6 FROM LINGUISTIC FEATURE TO GRAMMATICAL MODEL. WORDS, RHETORICAL FIGURES

I have now briefly glanced at some prominent models of grammar, not because they are the only ones that should be considered or the best, but because they show that different models may well prove to have different advantages in the linguistic description of style markers. In one model, a given area of grammar may have been more fully developed than in another; in one model, a set of stylistically relevant, and thus related, problems may have been kept together within one subsystem, whereas another model may have scattered them into different parts of the grammar and thus made their concentrated treatment more difficult.

There is, of course, another approach to the same problem: instead of taking a grammatical model and discussing how well suited it is to the description of certain types of potential style markers, we may take a number of style markers and then examine a number of different grammatical models to see how they might describe them. In fact, potential style markers can be found throughout the whole spectrum of language. They range from paralinguistic, phonetic, and phonemic features all the way through the lexis to the study of sentences, including word order and sentence length and complexity, and of textual as well as narrative units. A full discussion of such problems would therefore lead to a recapitulation of all of today's linguistics in the widest and most comprehensive sense. Once again, the following remarks amount to no more than a few hints at a few of many pertinent issues, beginning with a glance at lexicography.

A branch of stylolinguistic description conspicuous even to the non-linguist is the lexicographic categorization of words according to their stylistic value. Users of dictionaries are familiar with markings such as *colloq.*, *hist.* or *rhet.* Usually, however, such markings point out special terms — military, scientific, technical, historical, rhetorical, and so on — and the marking of stylistic values of more general words is less specific, though certain labels such as 'colloquial' or 'slang' are often used. I know of no dictionary that would have attempted an elaborate classification of contextual categories and a concomitant system of stylistic markings that would correlate with specific ranges of contexts. Rather, everyday experience suggests that any educated native speaker will be able to supplement dictionary entries with a wealth of further observations on the range of contexts in which a given word is most likely to occur. Today there is increasing agreement that dictionaries should not be compiled in a linguistic vacuum, that is, independently of linguistic theory. But the linguistic principles of lexicography tend to vary with each school of linguists — witness for instance the markings for strict subcategorization and for selection required by a lexicon in the model of CHOMSKY (1965) — and with each major theory. This may suggest that dictionaries marking frequent contextual ranges of occurrence should be produced especially for the needs of applied stylistics, for instance in foreign-language teaching. Frequency dictionaries — now usually produced by computer — can be excellent aids. Overall frequencies computed out of large samples tend to permit few conclusions as to the contextual range of words, but some frequency dictionaries (e.g. KUČERA – FRANCIS 1967) offer data by genre as well. Concordances, too, invite to the study of word frequencies in certain well-defined literary contexts. Some are devoted to restricted genres such as Old English poetry; more commonly, they cover the works of one great writer, usually a poet. In many stylistic problems, the great historical dictionaries with their wealth of examples (such as the Oxford English Dictionary) also offer some help. Nor should the student of style forget the special dictionaries of slang or of special subjects such as medicine or engineering, or the studies of special word fields (e.g. CROSLAND 1962; GLÄSER 1963, 1970a; GUILBERT 1965, 1968; LEECH 1966; WEXLER 1955). Students of older stages of languages might even profit from the markings of words in old dictionaries, which often reveal stylistic values and attitudes (OSSELTON 1958).

SIMILES, METONYMIES, METAPHORS, and other figures usually counted as rhetorical must not be left out from any list of potential style markers. Sometimes it suffices to reckon with their overall densities; often, however, a given style is characterized not merely by frequent metaphors but by a high density of certain specific types of metaphors. METAPHOR CLASSIFICATION will then become necessary (cf. BICKERTON 1969, PASINI 1968). Two main avenues are open here. Either we set up a syntactic taxonomy of metaphors in the manner of Christine BROOKE-ROSE, staying close to the syntactic surface (BROOKE-ROSE 1958). Or we operate with semantic matrices, trying to show what components of meaning the LITERAL TERM and the METAPHORIC TERM have in common. For instance, in *John is a lion*, both the literal *John* and the metaphoric *lion* are [+ noun], [+ animate], and, apparently, [+ brave]. But *John* is [+ human], *lion* is [− human]. We may proceed to label the set of semantic components that are shared by the literal and the metaphoric term (or, in terms of set theory, the intersection) as METAPHORIC CONSTRAINTS, and those different (the difference set) as METAPHORIC DIFFERENTIALS. In these terms we may find, for instance, that the style of a certain poet is characterized by a high density of certain specific metaphoric differentials. This high density becomes a style marker if it is significantly higher than the corresponding density in the norm against which we wish to view our poet's works. A frequent metaphoric differential in Emily Dickinson's poems, to take just one example, is [± divine]. Of course the student of style-marking metaphors will need a stringent apparatus of basic definitions. He must concern himself with points such as: if an expression of the type *x is y* is to qualify as a metaphor, the literal term *x* and the metaphoric term *y* must not be subsets one of the other. *John is a crusader* is thus not a metaphor if John belongs to the set of crusaders. But it becomes a metaphor if we presuppose that John is not a crusader, but for instance a pugnacious professor: pugnaciousness will then satisfy the requirement of metaphoric constraint, the difference between a real crusader and a pugnacious professor satisfying the requirement of metaphoric differential. This example was, by the way, chosen deliberately to illustrate how difficult some metaphoric con-

straints and differentials may be to verbalize in simple terms
of a matrix. Again, a student of style is likely to profit more
from fairly abstract categories such as [± divine] than from
very detailed, delicate ones that characterize single metaphors
rather than metaphor classes. Here, too, finding suitable
levels of delicacy and abstraction will be a crucial problem.
Nor should we forget that cultural and literary traditions play
an important rôle in specifying what kinds of metaphoric
constraints and differentials are permissible in a given culture,
language, and style. Some metaphors overlap with idioms in
refusing direct translation from one language into another.
Traditions also enter into specifying where runs the fine border
between a metaphor and a lie.

5.7 STYLES ACROSS LANGUAGES

I have here touched upon the question of styles across languages, which has theoretical as well as practical importance.
If we wish to study the similarities and the differences
between, say, legal style in English, French, and Russian, we
must have at our disposal a linguistic apparatus capable of
deciding what features in these different languages we must
regard as equivalent, and what features we must regard as
different. If, for instance, we wish to know whether legal English uses longer sentences than legal French, we must first know
whether all kinds of English perhaps use longer sentences
than all kinds of French. We shall, in other words, need a
comparison of English and French sentence length in more
general terms, and this comparison gives us the background
against which to view the results of our comparison of legal
English and legal French. Only if the results of the latter
comparison prove significantly different from the former are
we justified in regarding them as stylistic. Such comparisons
ought to be based on a theory of their own; otherwise they
readily become a series of unsystematic, scattered — though
perhaps interesting and suggestive — observations. Such

questions are highly relevant to the theory of translation (see e.g. CATFORD 1965, MOUNIN 1963, NIDA 1964), and also to practical translating. In fact, comparative stylistic studies of the languages involved would give us a welcome means of checking the stylistic accuracy of translations. Style is part of total meaning, and if a translator's aim is to make the text read as if it had been originally written in the target language, it must consistently follow the patterns of the style the original author would have used had he written in this, target, language, and lived within its culture.

5.8 STYLE AND RHETORIC.
ALLEGORY, IRONY, PARODY

Some potential style markers have been studied mainly by rhetoricians, and they sometimes need more stringent linguistic definition. Many examples could be cited of rhetorical devices that are potential style markers. One of them is the concept of the LOOSE SENTENCE, which can be interrupted before its end so that the part, or parts, before the interruption form a grammatical, acceptable sentence. The density of loose sentences might in fact be relatively easy to compute even out of relatively long texts. As Karl BOOST has shown, the cohesive tension within sentences differs, and is upheld by different means, in different languages (BOOST 1959). The English *Yesterday I bought a book in the shop* is thus inherently more loose — it can be interrupted after *book* — than the German *Gestern habe ich ein Buch in dem Laden gekauft*, in which the final verb functions as a signal upholding the tension and preventing earlier interruption. I have quoted this instance of contrastive English–German grammar to show another example of the risks of uncontrolled bilingual stylistics: figures on densities of loose sentences in English and German are not directly comparable as criteria of style, because these two languages have different methods of upholding cohesive tension within the sentence. Sentence looseness is also connected with embedding and with the left or right-branching structures described by YNGVE (1960), whose proportions may contribute to giving a text a conspicuous stylistic flavour.

So far, rhetoric has been more successful than strict grammar in dealing with textual units larger than the sentence. To what extent such units are amenable to strict linguistic definition is a very topical question whose dissection cannot be attempted here. In writing, the PARAGRAPH is a typographically marked unit, and therefore objectively verifiable. And in practice it is by no means impossible to use paragraph structure as a potential style marker. We may, for instance, proceed to count densities of paragraphs whose controlling idea is expressed in an initial topic sentence, paragraphs in which the controlling idea is implied rather than summarized in any one sentence, and paragraphs in which the controlling idea comes last. (See rhetorics such as BREWSTER 1912 and GENUNG 1900.)

When pushing upward towards larger textual units we are also approaching problems traditionally regarded as literary, not linguistic. Features such as allegory and irony will require a very sophisticated semantic apparatus before they become accessible to stringent, mechanical stylolinguistic description. ALLEGORY builds on the isomorphism between two simultaneous meanings of the text: the literal, surface meaning, and the allegorical, deep meaning. IRONY is based on a tension between a surface meaning and its opposite. In terms of the communication chain, irony might be described as a conspiracy between speaker/writer and listener/reader, both of whom know that a given textual unit should not be understood literally. This has to be signalled through special IRONY SIGNALS (WEINRICH 1966), which warn the receiver not to interpret certain sets of textual stimuli in their literal sense. Such irony signals need not be overtly present in a text. Some irony signals consist of contradictions of presupposed facts known to both communication partners, as in *Hitler was the kindest of men.* Others involve an inconsistency: if we are told that Chaucer's prioress only gave her dogs the finest of foods, and if we assume that many people were starving all around her and recall that it was the duty of nuns to help those in distress, we are predisposed to interpret Chaucer's praise of her gentility as irony. Irony signals may also be "exophoric" in that they refer to actions outside the text itself. If, in a play, we are shown that a character behaves horribly and then told that he is noble, the inconsistency between action and verbal characterization signals the irony. In speech, irony may be conveyed through specific patterns of stress and intonation and by paralinguistic means: rhythm, tempo, tone of voice, loudness, and the like. In writing, inverted commas are sometimes used as a crude kind of irony signal.

PARODIES are very often built around stylistic features. In fact one common kind of parody consists of a text with a very high, and perhaps exaggerated, density of the parodee's most conspicuous style markers. Non-discrete style markers, such as sentence length, may be given exaggerated values, too. The parodist's method is the verbal counterpart of caricature, where the artist seizes upon a few prominent features of his subject — a large nose and big ears, for instance — and exaggerates them so that they come to dominate his portrait. Similarly, the parodist's first task is to find a set of characteristic style markers, and then to compose a text with an exaggerated concentration of these very features. If the density of such imitated style markers is roughly the same as in the original, the result may be labelled as IMITATION or PASTICHE. (cf. IKEGAMI 1969)

5.9 TEXTUAL COMPLEXITY AND READABILITY

Some scholars have investigated characteristics of styles that consist, not of sets of single style markers but of complex resultants of many simultaneous style markers, sometimes in ways in which the single vectors are hard or impossible to disentangle. Examples of such complex style markers are TEXTUAL COMPLEXITY and READABILITY (WHO 1968, MILLER – COLEMAN 1967). Readability and textual complexity are influenced by many factors: the ease or difficulty of the vocabulary (which may roughly correlate with average word length); the ease or difficulty of clause and sentence structure (which should be measured not only in terms of sentence length but also of sentence complexity: ADMONI 1966, LESSKIS 1964); patterns of intersentence cohesion and connectivity in texts; the character and density of allusions and rhetorical figures; and the like. Textual complexity has been calibrated in its totality, without reference to the individual stimuli in the text, by methods such as cloze scores (obtained by having informants guess at words omitted from the text), answering questions on a passage, calculating distributional constraints and redundancy, and the like.

5.10 STYLISTICS AND CONTENT ANALYSIS

Stylistics also borders on CONTENT ANALYSIS (POOL 1959, ROSENGREN 1968, STONE 1966), especially those methods by which content analysts have investigated the densities of words and collocations in well-defined contexts. It should be noted that content analysis is not a single, hard-and-fast method but rather an approach in three steps. First, the investigator must limit his object of study. Secondly he must choose a sample according to explicit criteria. And, thirdly, he studies the frequency of certain objectively — and thus in practice linguistically — definable features in these materials through systematic counts and statistical controls. Both the student of style and the content analyst are thus interested in contextual densities of linguistic features. The difference is often one of purpose rather than method: content analysts choose their linguistic features, not because of their linguistic interest but because of their semantic content. Their basis is not linguistic but epistemological; the ultimate focus is on content, not on form, and forms are regarded not as entities in their own right but merely as reflections of content. The similarities between content analysis and the study of style are, however, sufficient to suggest that some of the content analysts' methods are potentially useful to students of style as well. Thus the co-occurrence of words that has often been studied by content analysts is also a potential style marker.

5.11 FROM STYLOLINGUISTICS TO LITERARY ANALYSIS

Above I listed four requirements for a linguistic model in stylolinguistic description. The model had to allow for variation and context. It had to be consistent. It had to be adequate. And it had to admit both categorical and probabilistic rules. In case it were not regarded as self-evident, we might now add a fifth requirement. Stylolinguistic methods have to be objective in the sense that anybody who repeats the analysis of the same materials by the same methods must arrive at the same result. The concepts and definitions must be operationally concrete and unambiguous. As long as we use modern, strict grammatical models as the basis of our stylolinguistic description, this requirement is easy to satisfy. But if we venture into those areas that are important for stylistics but which so far lie in the margin of, or even beyond, linguistics proper, we must watch the integrity of our concepts and methods. When we are dealing with rhetorical or literary features, with metaphor, irony, and the like, the temptation to relax the rigour of the apparatus will be overwhelming. To yield to such temptations is, of course, not a sin. Actually, it may be the only way in which some jobs will get done at all. Indeed we may, at the present stage of linguistics, be compelled to give up the demands that a strict methodology puts on operational concreteness and rigorous conceptual frames. But we should then be aware that our investigation stops being stylolinguistic and becomes something else, for instance, literary criticism, where brilliant intuitions and elegant, often metaphoric, verbalizations of subjective responses are at a premium. In comparison, linguistic stylistics of the stricter kind often seems a highly pedestrian subject.

To illustrate some of the grammatical categories that stylolinguists have counted I shall, finally, refer to a few examples of quantitative studies. These examples will also support the observation that, though modern linguistics offers many highly sophisticated and subtle concepts and approaches, in stylistics a relatively simple and traditional grammar can go a long way.

An excellent example is Louis T. MILIC's computer study of Swift's style (MILIC 1967). MILIC studied Swift's seriation, including percentages of doublets and triplets, sequences of words and groups of words, normal and asyndetic and polysyndetic series, series with a continuator such as *etc.*, and so on. His report contains another section on Swift's connectives: sentence-initial co-ordinating conjunctions, subordinating conjunctions, and conjunctive adverbs. The most elaborate part of MILIC's analyses was concerned with word-classes and word-class distribution. Among the statistical characteristics are the proportion of function words; the "Stable Style Characteristic" computed with the aid of values for four groups of frequencies, namely those of verbals, finite verbs and auxiliaries, modals, and connectives; ratios between nominals and verbals, adjectives, and verbs; and the occurrence of different three-word patterns within the sentence (which a computer can readily be programmed to identify and count). As MILIC concludes, these features, all of which can be easily defined with the aid of a relatively elementary grammar, suffice to show a whole set of style markers by which Swift's style differs from the styles of Addison, Johnson, Gibbon, and Macaulay. The burden lies on the statistics. All the linguistics MILIC really needed was a basic grammar capable of adequate definitions of series, conjunctions, and word classes.

Richard OHMANN's study of Shaw (OHMANN 1962) is different in appearance: it shows how a primarily literary analysis can gain support from statistical counts, and how a body of statistical data can be presented without fanfare in a slender appendix. Those who prefer readability to statistics should seek comfort in OHMANN's combination of a sensitive, elegant essay and a sound method. The essay concentrates on connections between Shaw's literary qualities and his language. The first appendix gives comparative counts of samples of some 2,500 words out of Shaw, Yeats, Bertrand Russell, the Webbs, Chesterton, and Oscar Wilde — in other words, from a contextually related norm. The features OHMANN counts are long series, comparatives, *would*, all-or-nothing determiners and degree words as well as degree intensity, extent, limits, and quantity; appositions, negatives, direction shifts, requests, dependent clauses, quotations, introductory *that*, references to beliefs and to statements and propositions, proper names, personal pronouns, the proportion of person words among grammatical subjects, mental causation, infinitives, abstract nouns, and adjectives. The list is remarkable for its blend of very different types of units. As OHMANN himself has emphasized, some of the categories were defined more by feel than by exact linguistic rule; he may thus have overstepped the bounds of strict linguistics. Also the sample, though carefully chosen, was too small to permit confident statistical generalizations. In the respects considered, all the other writers still proved more like one another than any one of them was like Shaw. OHMANN's conclusion is that

a small but carefully selected group of counts is more useful in isolating the style of a writer than would be a much larger but randomly chosen group (OHMANN 1962: 185).

The second appendix is devoted to a study of revisions in some of Shaw's typescripts, and it shows that revisions are particularly frequent precisely within those areas that are of particular relevance to Shaw's style.

Walker GIBSON is one of the students of style who have attempted setting up statistical frames for the diagnosis of styles, not only descriptions of single styles. (GIBSON 1966) Though written in a light vein with a somewhat cavalier approach to statistics, GIBSON's book — appropriately labelled *Tough, Sweet and Stuffy* — suggests a battery of statistical tests for the distinction of three major styles in modern American prose. GIBSON began by classifying a number of texts under each of his three impressionistic headings, 'tough', 'sweet', and 'stuffy'. He then studied each group to see what its texts had in common. To give just a few examples of GIBSON's criteria: a 'tough' text has more than 70 per cent monosyllables and less than 10 per cent words of 3 syllables or more; a 'stuffy' text has a maximum of 60 per cent monosyllables and 20 per cent or more of words of at least 3 syllables. Texts with values between 'tough' and 'stuffy' are 'sweet'. A text with more than one passive per 5 verbs is stuffy, one with less than one passive per 20 verbs is tough, and one with no passives at all is sweet. GIBSON finally gives a set of ten rules how to avoid being stuffy, which — characteristically — ends with a tenth commandment: "Don't obey all these rules at once !" GIBSON is no doubt right in claiming that the profiles that emerge out of measuring a text with his quantitative tests do indicate some general stylistic characteristics of that text. The recognition of three major styles was, of course, based entirely on GIBSON's initial intuition. But it would be interesting to study a corpus of texts more thoroughly and see how far GIBSON's intuitions are supportable by factor analysis and numerical taxonomy.

In a study of over 60,000 sentences brought from 30 German texts out of four genres (plays, fictional prose, factual prose, scientific prose), Werner WINTER similarly restricted himself to three comparatively simple, rapidly countable criteria: sentence-initial parts of speech, clause length, and sentence complexity (WINTER 1961). There was a clear correlation between context and the frequencies of some of these features.

The density of sentences that begin with adverbials was higher in written, and particularly in scientific, prose than in plays, which were here taken to reflect patterns of spoken German. The density of finite verbs per total number of words was low in scientific prose and higher in plays and in fiction, with a great deal of scatter in factual prose. These findings can be reinterpreted as contextual probabilities, which can be read both from context to linguistic density, and from linguistic density to context. In written German, about 35 per cent of all sentences began with adverbials; in primarily spoken German, only 17.5 per cent did. Thus if we take a scientific text in German, we are likely to find that some 35 per cent of its sentences begin with adverbials, whereas, the other way round, if we find that a text has 35 per cent sentence-initial adverbials, we may predict that this will contribute to giving it a scientific flavour.

The comparison between text and norm need not be synchronic as in the studies of MILIC, OHMANN, GIBSON, and WINTER. An example of a comparison between texts from the same contextual sphere but from different periods is Lars GRAHN's pilot study of Swedish newspaper styles (GRAHN 1965). A study of 85 articles from *Dagens Nyheter* in 1890 (41,753 words) and of 124 articles from the same newspaper in 1964 (83,760 words) showed that the average length of sentences had shrunk from 24.39 words in 1890 to 17.49 words in 1964. The greatest difference, a shift from 35.45 to 20.38 words per sentence, was found in the leaders; the smallest, from 13.80 to 13.72 words per sentence, in *causeries*. The number of embedded subordinate clauses per 1,000 running words of text had similarly diminished from 6.61 in 1890 to 3.96 in 1964. The relations between different contextual genres had also changed. In 1890, cultural articles had the greatest density of embedded subordinate clauses; by 1964, they had fewer embedded subordinate clauses than leaders and foreign news reports. Comparable differences, both between the styles of 1890 and 1964 and between the styles of different genres

first in 1890 and then in 1964, were also found in the densities
of attributive participles, participles embedded between
genitive attribute and head, and some other syntactic structures. Altogether, GRAHN's figures offer ample statistical
reasons why Swedish newspapers of 1890, and especially some
subcategories of their text, strike modern readers as 'heavy'.

5.12 SUMMARY

Many, no less successful and suggestive reports could be cited,
and many more will no doubt be forthcoming in the near
future. But these must suffice. They show concrete examples
of a number of statements made in the course of my essay on
defining style (ENKVIST – SPENCER – GREGORY 1964) and repeated in this book. They all relate texts to contexts. Then
they compare the densities of selected linguistic features in
the text with the corresponding densities in a contextually
definable, related, and suitably contrastive norm — suitably
contrastive, that is, to bring out the desired stylistic differential. For Swift, MILIC found a suitable norm in Addison,
Johnson, Gibbon, and Macaulay; for Shaw, OHMANN chose a
norm from Yeats, Bertrand Russell, the Webbs, Chesterton,
and Wilde; GIBSON compared three categories of texts;
WINTER contrasted primarily written and primarily spoken
texts; and GRAHN worked with the same newspaper from 1890
and 1964. In every instance, the norm was carefully chosen
for its definite contextual relationship with the text. And
those features whose density in the text was found to be
significantly different from the density of the corresponding
features in the norm were regarded as stylistic characteristics,
or style markers, for that text. Once the correspondence
between style markers and contextual ranges had been
established, it could be made use of both ways: if we know the
style markers we may draw conclusions about the context,
and if we know the context we may predict what types of

style markers are likely to occur in it. The former, diagnostic procedure was used by GIBSON to classify texts, and it forms the basis of stylistic author determination which I shall discuss in a later chapter. The latter is the approach we use when characterizing the language that occurs in given contexts, for instance when discussing the styles of authors, genres, or periods. Finally, all the five studies cited made good use of relatively simple grammatical features (which OHMANN supplemented with a few complex and subjective ones without attempting complex and stringent linguistic definitions). Even such simple features proved operationally adequate to bring out inventories of style markers.

6

DEVIANCE

6.1 DEVIANCE

One of the areas in which linguists have gained in sophistication is the study of GRAMMATICALITY, or GRAMMATICAL WELL-FORMEDNESS. This area is relevant to students of style on two counts. First, certain texts — modern poems, for instance — achieve some of their stylistic effects precisely by departing from the ordinary norms of well-formedness. If we are to describe their style in linguistic terms, we need a theory and method of description of the ways in which a text can depart from normal usage. Secondly, all styles must, by definition, be regarded as "deviant" — not necessarily from normal patterns of well-formedness, but from contextually definable norms and thus from other styles. The former type of deviance, which is the focus of this chapter, results from actual tinkering with the rules of normal grammar. The latter results from the fact that the features of normal language and the rules of normal grammar are used with different densities in the generation of different texts. As we have seen, such "well-formed" styles can be explained by the comparison of densities of well-formed features in the text with the corresponding densities in a suitable, contextually related norm.

6.2 GRAMMATICALITY, ACCEPTABILITY, TOLERANCE

Another very important type of deviance is the normal and acceptable ungrammaticality of spontaneous, unscripted speech. In fact, this kind of deviance was one of the motives for the introduction into linguistics of concepts such as *parole* and performance. Studies such as BOWMAN (1966) and Lo-MAN – JÖRGENSEN (1971) have pinpointed a number of problems that analysts of deviant patterns in spoken styles have to face. One of them concerns the definition of the basic unit of spoken language. In speech, people often express themselves in units which do not satisfy the requirements of grammatical sentences, for instance in sentence fragments. Therefore the analyst of spoken language will have to develop an apparatus capable of segmenting a text into suitable syntactic units, some of which do not qualify as well-formed sentences. BOWMAN has divided utterances into sentences, which are marked by intonation contours and terminal juncture, and fragments, which are interrupted; sentences are further subdivided into major sentences containing both subject and predicate, and minor sentences (BOWMAN 1966). LOMAN and his co-workers operate with macrosyntagms, which can be subclassified as follows:

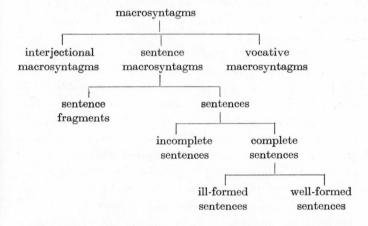

Fragments are defined as sentences lacking a finite verb in the main clause, whereas incomplete sentences lack a contextually relevant constituent at the end of the sentence (aposiopesis). Ill-formed sentences can be subclassified by type of deviance. Such types are anacoluthon, self-correction on a syntactic level, omission of a syntactically relevant part of the clause, attempts at continuing an already complete sentence, and interruptions (EINARSSON 1971: 32, 118; JÖRGENSEN 1971).

As terms such as *grammaticality* and *well-formedness* have been used in different senses, their user owes his audience a definition. I shall here use *grammaticality* simply to indicate the extent to which a given sentence has been formed according to the rules of a given grammar. If the grammar G generates the sentence S, S is GRAMMATICAL, or, synonymously, WELL–FORMED with respect to grammar G. If grammar G has been set up hierarchically so that it has a set of ordered rules, some of which are more fundamental, or deeper, than others, we can set up a scale of grammaticality. Sentences that violate more fundamental, deeper rules are less grammatical than sentences that violate less basic rules that lie closer to the surface. ACCEPTABILITY, on the other hand, is a concept relative not to a given grammar but to the opinion of an informant or group of informants. Within this terminology it is therefore perfectly possible to write a grammar of a language which generates unacceptable sentences: in terms of the grammar, they are grammatical and well-formed, even if a group of informants rejects them as unacceptable. Conversely, informants may accept sentences not generated by the grammar. Such sentences are acceptable but, in terms of our grammar, ungrammatical. Like grammaticality, acceptability can be scaled: if all of one hundred suitably selected informants agree on accepting a given sentence, this sentence has a higher acceptability than a sentence which is only accepted by half of the informants. In practice, groups of informants can be far from unanimous when judging the acceptability of certain types of structures. This suggests that grammaticality, which is an absolute and can be defined in terms of a given set of rules, and acceptability, which is relative to informant opinion, will never fully agree (QUIRK – SVARTVIK

1966, GREENBAUM – QUIRK 1970). We therefore need both concepts (Cf. CHOMSKY 1965).

Acceptability does not, however, exist in a situational vacuum. Informants may accept a given sentence in one context (including situation) and reject the same sentence in another. I shall use the term *tolerance* for 'acceptability in a given context'. Thus in the context of modern poetry, *anyone lived in a pretty how town* is tolerated, though in the context of factual prose it would be unacceptable and though it is ungrammatical in the light of ordinary grammars of English. Each context is in fact characterized by a TOLE-RANCE RANGE or MARGIN OF TOLERANCE. Certain rituals in armies, the Church, and other tradition-bound establish-ments may have no tolerance margin in the sense that their language is "frozen" (JOOS 1962) to certain fixed expressions. In other contexts, the range of tolerance may be very wide, even wide enough to permit verbal play. I already noted this above in section *1.6* in connection with context parameters.

Finally, I shall use the term DEVIANCE to indicate the differ-ence between a text and the overall grammatical norm of the language. Deviance is thus the sum of nongrammaticality and nonacceptability, and a blanket term covering two poten-tially different factors. However, here *deviance* does not in-clude those non-deviant styles that arise through differences in densities of well-formed features in a text and a contextu-ally related norm; *deviance* thus does not have the second of the senses referred to in the first paragraph of this chapter.

6.3 TRANSFORMATIONALIST AND BEHAVIOURIST VIEWS OF WELL-FORMEDNESS

It should perhaps be noted that the need for distinctions not only between "right" and "wrong" but between degrees of grammaticality and acceptability has arisen both in trans-formational grammar and in large studies of actual usage.

In all work with generative grammars we are compelled to test the output. When writing the grammar we set up a tentative sequence of rules that generate a set of sentences. We must then decide whether these sentences are desirable or not. If they are, our rules may stand; if they are not, we must revise the rules. In practice, writing a generative grammar involves very large numbers of such decisions. Processes of this kind have contributed greatly to sharpening our views of deviant expressions and evaluations of their degrees of grammaticality and acceptability. Obviously, acceptability and tolerance are, in a sense, more fundamental than grammaticality. Grammars are written by linguists, who can manipulate their grammaticality scales; acceptability and tolerance reside in a collective *Sprachgefühl* and can only be influenced indirectly through changes in usage and style. Of course a grammarian should all the same test the output of his grammar against some strict norms of acceptability and tolerance, even if these are merely the ones of his own idiolect and of his own subjective sense of linguistic and stylistic propriety.

In general, behaviourist structuralists found deviance an awkward concept. The reasons seem clear enough. They based their linguistic descriptions on explicitly defined corpora of texts, and they insisted on the use of immanent categories actually present on the surface of the text, without permitting judgments as to degrees of correctness or grammaticality in the text itself. Thus if the corpus contained a deviant expression, that expression had to be incorporated into the description precisely in the same way as a non-deviant expression. Now if, say, a grammarian decided to include the poems of E. E. Cummings, their structures became part of modern English and thus non-deviant. If, again, the grammarian decided to exclude them and put them into a separate grammar of Cummingsese, that grammar had to be immanent, that is, based not on categories of non-Cummingsian English but on Cummingsese alone. Now if Cummingsese is described as a new and separate language, its categories may well become very different from those of normal English, especially if the grammarian uses criteria of maximal descriptive economy in his description of Cummingsese. The grammar of Cummingsese runs the risk of becoming hard to compare with that of non-deviant English. Yet we well know that Cummings's poems are not effective in a vacuum. Their effect, our intuition tells us, is founded not on their form as such, but rather on our knowing how each of Cummings's expressions differs from a comparable set of related expressions in non-deviant English. Altogether, the effect of deviant poetry is based on comparisons between deviant and normal expressions.

6.4 GRAMMATICALITY SCALES

The density of deviant structures may be a style marker in its own right, like the density of metaphors. But just as one poet's style may differ from that of another, not by an overall density of metaphor but by densities of different types of metaphors, so one deviant text may differ from another deviant text because of different kinds of deviance. Cummings's deviance is not the same as Lewis Carroll's. We therefore need a classification of different types of deviance.

One starting-point for such a classification is the ranking of deviant expressions on a scale of grammaticality, which becomes possible as soon as we have a generative grammar with ordered rules. In terms of generative-transformational grammar, a string such as *a who the of today would be found to violate some very basic rules and thus to be greatly ungrammatical. In *I thermometer you, the deviance results from use of a substantive where normal grammar requires a verb. In *I elapsed the book to her we are using a verb, elapse, in a structure reserved for certain other verbs such as give, and thus breaking what one transformational model (CHOM-

SKY 1965) called "strict subcategorization rules". And in
The stone snores, the ungrammaticality consists of a breach
of a "selection rule" which says that animate verbs such as
snore require animate subjects, not inanimate ones such as
stone. (Breaches of selection rules may result in metaphor.)
There will, however, be a residue of sentences such as the
famous *Both of John's parents are married to aunts of mine*,
which are hard to diagnose as deviant in grammatical terms
unless we incorporate into our grammars a semantic component capable of blocking these logical absurdities. How this
should be done is a controversial question.

6.5 STRATEGIES IN THE DESCRIPTION OF DEVIANT
TEXTS

Devices such as those exemplified above will suggest ways
to describe different patterns of deviance in more precise
terms. We should, however, still face the question of what
method we ought to prefer when describing a deviant text.
At least three alternative strategies seem to be available
(LEVIN 1963, 1965a; THORNE 1965, 1969, 1970; HENDRICKS
1969).

First, if we have a full generative grammar of the language
at our disposal, we may note at what point the deviant
structure departs from the normal sequence of generative
rules. In terms of the above examples, *I elapse the book*
would be less grammatical than *The stone snores*. Secondly,
we may regard the deviant text as having been written in a
different language. We may then proceed to write a grammar
of this new language. If we do so, our new grammar is likely
to generate not only the particular sentences of our original,
deviant text, but a large — and perhaps infinite — number of
other texts as well. Such overgeneration is not, however,
necessarily an evil: these other, "overgenerated" texts may

afford interesting examples of the type of deviation we are
concerned with. They are, in a sense, imitations or pastiches
of the original. If, for instance, we write a grammar for Cummings, a generative rule allowing *he danced his did* is likely to
generate not only those sentences of this type that Cummings
actually used, but also a number he did not use, such as *he
ran his ate* or *he wrote his slept*. And a generative rule permitting Dylan Thomas's *a grief ago* might also generate *a ciga-
rette ago* and, perhaps, *three husbands ago*. The more basic
the deviant rule, the larger the number of overgenerated
structures. The risk of this second approach is that the
grammar written for the deviant text may depart too
far from the grammar of non-deviant language. We must
therefore take care to formulate constraints compelling us
to make the deviant grammar conform sufficiently closely
to that of non-deviant language. We shall need a theory for
such restraints.

The third strategy is, in a sense, the most interesting because it tries to incorporate the actual process of interpretation of deviant structures. Here we again take for granted that
we have a full grammar of the non-deviant language at our
disposal. When faced with a deviant structure, we interpret
it by associating it with that structure, or perhaps those
structures, in the non-deviant language which we feel to
be its nearest equivalents. To cite KATZ:

The speaker's understanding of the [deviant] semi-sentence is nothing
other than his understanding of the sentences in the [non-deviant]
set with which the semi-sentence is associated (FODOR – KATZ 1964:
411).

Our description of the deviant sentence will thus come to
consist of a set of normal sentences that we might call its
COMPREHENSION SET, and a set of rules which explain precisely
how the deviant sentence is associated with each of the sentences of the comprehension set. Such TRANSFER RULES will

also throw light on the reasons why a given comprehension set, and not another, was associated with a given deviant sentence. This model in fact suggests active experiments with informants to show with what degree of agreement different people can offer comprehension sets for specific instances and types of deviance.

6.6 CLOSED TEXTS, OPEN TEXTS, AND CHOICES OF GRAMMATICAL MODELS

William S. CHISHOLM has posed a question that we should now try to answer. "Is it," he asked "necessary to have a reserve of all sentences in order to describe a few? Or, to put it differently, is a generative grammar the one that stylistics needs?" (CHISHOLM 1967: 26)

If style is a result of a comparison of frequencies in two closed texts — a CLOSED TEXT being a text which is available in its entirety and an OPEN TEXT being a text which may be added to — we may in principle choose between a taxonomic and a generative model. For taxonomic models are also capable of describing closed texts. If, however, the norm, or both text and norm, are open, we must use a grammar which is adequate for the description of open texts and which can predict what occurs even beyond the actually available sample or samples. And if we suspect that our text may use deviant structures as style markers, the requirement of adequacy speaks strongly for the use of a generative model. For here, adequacy requires a description of generative processes rather than of surface structures: the densities of deviant structures as such may not suffice. We may need subclassifications of different types of deviant structures that are based on depth of deviance, and this presupposes a generative grammar with ordered rules. But whatever model we use, it must be capable of allowing comparisons of densities of linguistic features.

Such arguments may be modified by working hypotheses, however. Not infrequently, linguists have tacitly assumed

that an open corpus such as modern English may be described
in terms of a closed text, which is then regarded as a representative sample of the open corpus. And even in their work
with closed texts, linguists are usually interested in those
underlying general patterns that allow predictions beyond
the text itself. If a linguist studies Old English poetry, for
instance, he is not only interested in the surface of the poems
but also, and perhaps even more, in the set of rules that Old
English poets used when composing their poems. He thus
operates with the hypothesis that his corpus is in fact open
and comprises all of the actual and potential poems in Old
English, even though he only has a sample of actual, surviving poems at his disposal. This is one of the basic differences
between most linguists and most literary scholars. The latter
generally study closed texts for their uniqueness, whereas
linguists are often committed to regarding them as samples
that help them to discover the underlying patterns and rule
systems that were applied to their generation. In linguistic
stylistics, decisions as to whether text and norm should be
regarded as closed or as open follow from the choice of text
and norm. In work with closed texts, densities may take the
form of actual numbers of occurrence; in work with open texts,
we must reckon with probabilities computed from that closed
body of text which we regard as our sample.

6.7 GENERATIVE-TRANSFORMATIONAL METHODS
IN THE COMPARISON OF LANGUAGE VARIANTS

Yet another question should be mentioned. If we compare
two variants of a language in terms of generative grammar,
in what form should we express our results? I emphasized above that two variants of a language may differ in
two ways. First, if both use the same set of rules, but
with different patterns of frequency, we must somehow
attach to each rule a measure of the frequency with which

it is used in each variant. OHMANN did this by listing the transformations of closed texts together with their frequencies, whereas LABOV extended the method to open texts by setting up probabilistic rules with variable input (see above, sections *3.3* and *5.3*). Secondly, if the two variants use different rules, we may proceed to classify such rule differences into a few definite subtypes. Thus one or the other variant may have a rule which is missing from the other grammar. Two otherwise identical rules may be differently ordered in the two grammars. Two rules in the two grammars may apply to the same feature but rewrite it differently: one grammar rewrites $x \rightarrow y \mid A - B$, the other $x \rightarrow z/A - B$. Finally, two grammars may have rules with the same structural change but their sphere of application can be different. Such differences between related grammars have so far been studied mainly by those interested in historical syntax (KIPARSKY 1968, TRAUGOTT 1965), but their methods are potentially applicable to the comparison of any related grammars, including those of stylistic variants of the same language.

6.8 PSYCHOLINGUISTIC APPROACHES TO DEVIANCE

Just as a number of style markers can be packaged and studied collectively under labels such as "complexity" or "readability", total patterns of deviance have also been analysed by psycholinguistic methods (CHAPMAN 1968, DANKS 1969). At least in some situations, informants are able to scale deviant sentences in accord with formal criteria of grammaticality, and the ease of learning and recall increase with increasing grammaticality. Meaningfulness, however, can sometimes be scaled independently of grammaticality. Such findings are interesting, but the experiments have so far used comparatively rough methods when making up the deviant sentences for the experiments. Thus words of grammatical sentences have been scrambled randomly, or deviant sentences have been created by writing a number of sentences with similar surface structures under each other and then reading the resulting matrix diagonally. The experiments might well gain in linguistic and stylistic relevance if methods could be devised to set up deviant sentences with an improved control not only of the rough level of grammaticality, but also of the number and type of transfer rules needed to make each test sentence grammatical. For it may well be rash to assume that depth of deviance is the only factor affecting the meaningfulness of the deviant sentence. Meaningfulness may also be affected by other factors such as the complexity of the transfer from deviant to normal: a transfer close to the surface, but requiring many transfer rules, may perhaps rank high on a scale of transfer complexity, and make the deviant sentence difficult to understand.

LINGUISTIC STYLE MARKERS
BEYOND THE SENTENCE

7.1 STYLE AS A QUALITY OF TEXTS

In their quest for simple definitions that could be hung on the pegs of well-established linguistic concepts, some scholars tried to equate style with the linguistics of *parole*. Just as simple are the definitions of style as the linguistics of units larger than the sentence (HILL 1958: 406). Such views have, however, also been contradicted by style theorists emphasizing the role of the sentence as a style carrier (OHMANN 1967).

If definitions of style were rigidly restricted to features involving spans larger than the sentence, they would lead to difficulties. First, even single sentences have a style, and stylistic incongruities such as the use of a colloquial word in an otherwise solemn, high-style frame may occur within the bounds of one sentence. And the other way round: quite a few features of textual cohesion between sentences can be regarded as grammatical rather than as stylistic. Pronominal references, concord, and certain other grammatical phenomena do not stop at sentence borders. Indeed, in some languages, for instance Czech and Russian, the structure makes the word order of sentences strongly sensitive to their textual environment (ADAMEC 1966; BUTTKE 1963, 1969; FIRBAS 1964a; KOVTUNOVA 1969). In fact, the old, tacit assumption that grammars deal with sentences has been honoured in the breach as well as in the observance. In traditional grammar, the apparatus was so formless and flexible that problems of text linguistics could intrude freely into a discussion ostensibly devoted to sentences rather than to texts. In more highly formalized grammatical models such as generative-transformational grammar, the introduction of textual features becomes explicit and therefore conspicuous. It may take the form of PRESUPPOSITIONS, or of special INTERSENTENCE FORMATIVES such as the [± mentioned] which is attachable to noun phrases to govern the choice of syntactic function (such as theme or subject), of the choice of article (indefinite or definite), and of certain phonological patterns (NICKEL 1970).

The need for text linguistics has thus become obvious within sentence grammar: certain features of sentences cannot be described, or correctly generated, without reference to intersentence features and to portions of the text beyond the sentence under consideration. At the same time, the study of discourses and texts has led to a new branch of linguistics which expressly devotes itself to text spans larger than the sentence. (BENSE 1962, 1969; VAN DIJK 1970a, 1970b; HARWEG 1968; HENDRICKS 1968; KARLSEN 1959; KINNANDER 1959; KLOEPFER – OOMEN 1970; KOCH 1966, 1970; MEL'ČUK – ŽOLKOVSKIJ 1970; PETŐFI 1970; SGALL 1969; STEMPEL 1971; etc.) There is an obvious area of overlap between studies in text linguistics, which approach single sentences as parts of larger units, and that part of grammar which studies cohesion devices in terms of sentences (e.g. HASAN 1968). Those who wish to keep these overlapping areas apart may give them separate labels and, for instance, distinguish between TEXT LINGUISTICS and INTERSENTENCE GRAMMAR. The former is mainly preoccupied with texts, the latter with those features of sentences that require reference beyond the sentence itself. Text linguistics is thus a discipline in its own right, whereas intersentence grammar is a necessary part of "ordinary" sentence grammar.

7.2 TEXTUAL WELL-FORMEDNESS,
TEXTUAL ACCEPTABILITY, TEXTUAL TOLERANCE

Some of the most fundamental problems of these branches of linguistics emerge from a contemplation of a RANDOM SENTENCE STRING:

> .John is a boy. Not yet, but you soon will. If we examine the wave form in figure 4.6, we can see that, while the sound lasts, peaks of pressure occur every thousandth of a second. Good morning. At the beginning of Queen Victoria's reign, many Londoners were very poor. Its invention is commonly ascribed to the late Nicholas Longworth. He will be an ideal companion for a night at Las Vegas.

Here every sentence is grammatical as well as acceptable when taken in isolation. Still anybody who knows English will classify the passage as textually ill-formed: the succession of these individual sentences seems odd, and the sentences will not be tolerated in this particular textual environment, though they would be perfectly all right in certain other environments. One might note in passing that the study of such random sentence strings is by no means uninteresting. By trying to spot the features that make them textually ill-formed we may gather clues as to what characteristics are necessary if a sentence string is to qualify as a well-formed text. This should also remind us of the well-known fact that in many situations, people go to great lengths to make sense of sentence strings that seem queer at first sight. And this is true not only of strings of sentences but of strings of other elements as well: many metaphors, for instance, require the receiver to devote considerable effort to their interpretation. Only if no hypotheses as to possible cohesion can be maintained are we willing to give up, and either to dismiss the text as deviant beyond reason, or, more humbly, to acknowledge our own shortcomings as interpreters.

There does, then, seem to be a quality of TEXTUAL WELL-FORMEDNESS or TEXTUALITY which corresponds to the grammatical well-formedness or grammaticality of sentence linguistics. In this sense, the ability of distinguishing between textually well-formed and textually ill-formed sentence strings seems to be part of each speaker's internalization of linguistic patterns, and thus part of his total linguistic competence. Again, if we adopt the view that all features of competence must be placed within the domain of grammar, it seems hard to escape the conclusion that a complete grammar ought to offer explicit criteria not only for the grammaticality of single sentences, but also for textual well-formedness. We may similarly extend our definitions not only of well-formedness, that is, of conformity to the explicit rules of our grammar, but also of acceptability and of tolerance, to the textual domain. In addition to textuality we should then speak of TEXTUAL ACCEPTABILITY and of TEXTUAL TOLERANCE, as well as of TEXTUAL DEVIANCE. In analogy with grammatical acceptability, textual acceptability should be studied through elicitation experiments with informants, though at the textual level such experiments will inevitably turn much more complex, perhaps forbiddingly so.

Textual tolerance can exist at two levels. First, a sentence acceptable in one place — for instance in the middle — of a text may not be tolerated in another place, for instance as a text-initial sentence: the place of a sentence in a string of sentences may require that sentence to satisfy certain textual requirements. Secondly, a string of sentences may satisfy the demands of textual acceptability in one context but not in another. For instance, the string

> The girl was liked since she was pretty. Since she was pretty the girl was liked. The girl, since she was pretty, was liked. The girl was poor if pretty. The girl, if pretty, was poor. If pretty, the girl was poor.

is presumably within the tolerance margin of its actual context, a grammar-book offering illustrations for the rule "*If* and *since* convert one subject-predicate group into a movable modifier of another". It might perhaps be tolerated in some literary contexts — one thinks of Gertrude Stein — but its repetitions and permutations would probably make people regard it as textually ill-formed if it occurred for instance in a legal context, where repetitions obey a different set of intersentential and intrasentential rules. Thus tolerance in the sense of 'context-bound acceptability' seems relevant to text linguistics as well.

7.3 TEXTUAL DEVIANCE AS A STYLE MARKER

Just as the use of deviant patterns of sentence grammar is a frequent device with poets such as Cummings or, in Swedish, Gunnar Björling, so prose writers and dramatists occasionally use odd, and perhaps deviant, textual patterns for literary effect. In *Hamlet* II.ii, Polonius is rightly puzzled by thematic jumps in Hamlet's speech, though he suspects that "though this be madness, yet there is method in't". In Ionesco, breaches of textual tolerance presumably symbolize the absurdities of life; in *La chantatrice chauve*, some of them result from the contextual transfer of sets of sentences from a linguistic phrase-book into real-life situations. And in some of Harold Pinter's dialogues, the relations between successive lines seem contrived to illustrate how difficult it is for one human being to achieve contact with another. Pinter's means are, however, more subtle and not as patently deviant as those of Hamlet's mad phase, Ionesco, or experimentators such as Gertrude Stein. Interior monologue and stream-of-consciousness prose are also examples of texts in which the patterns used to link sentences often differ from those that occur in expository prose.

The use of textually deviant sentence strings in certain contexts supports the view that the manner in which sentences are strung together into texts may also function as a style marker. In linguistic stylistics we should therefore try to develop concepts and frames for the description of different types of sentence sequences, whose range of occurrence could be studied in terms of context categories. If certain patterns of sentence sequence are significantly more frequent in a given text than in a norm chosen for its contextual relationship with that text, they qualify as style markers precisely like any other linguistic features.

7.4 THEME AND RHEME. THEME DYNAMICS. COHESION DEVICES

To develop an apparatus for the description of patterns of sentence sequence we shall do wisely in beginning not only from ordinary syntax but also from the studies of theme that have been developed notably by the Prague linguists (MATHE-SIUS, FIRBAS, DANEŠ, ADAMEC), by HALLIDAY (1967–68), and some others (e.g. DAHL 1969). The basic observations that suggested such studies concerned word order as a result of various system of organization. In English, the basic linguistic task of word order is to mark the function of groups in the sentence: in *John kicked Jack* and *Jack kicked John*, we identify subject and object by position before and after the verb. In languages where these functions are marked by case endings, word-order patterns may be free to express other functions such as those of THEME or TOPIC or, roughly, what is talked about, and RHEME or COMMENT or what is said about it. An additional distinction is that between GIVEN or DATUM, which has been mentioned before in the text, and NEW or NOVUM, which has not. Often, but not always, the theme consists of what is given, and the rheme of what is new. In Russian and Czech, for instance, these criteria of FUNCTIO-NAL SENTENCE PERSPECTIVE are fundamental factors in determining word order. In English, where word order is partially tied to functions such as subject and object, certain other devices are used to indicate functional sentence perspective.

Passives may thus make themes out of objects of transitive verbs by lifting them into the sentence-initial position which usually identifies themes. Other structures such as introductory *there*, the cleft construction of the type *It was x that did y*, and the inversion that allows sentences to begin with thematic adverbials *(In London once lived a witch)* may be viewed as part of the machinery of functional sentence perspective in English.

It would take another book to discuss the present state of knowledge of this intricate subject. We cannot here analyse connections between THEMATIZATION and EMPHASIS, the marking of themes and of textual patterns in spoken language by means of stress and intonation and other features, the correlation between theme and the use of the definite article, the various instances in which non-initial themes may occur, and the like. At present the discussion is further complicated by the fact that different scholars do not always agree about the definitions of basic concepts and terms such as *theme* and *rheme*, *topic* and *comment*, and *given* and *new*. All the same the problems of thematization are now beginning to assume their rightful place in linguistics as one of the systems necessary to explain the form of sentences and of texts.

In intersentence grammar as well as in text linguistics, we cannot rest satisfied with a linguistic apparatus only capable of discussing the statics of themes and rhemes within single sentences. On the contrary, we shall need a THEME DYNAMICS expressly designed for descriptions of patterns of thematic cohesion in a string of sentences. In other words, theme dynamics charts the patterns by which themes recur in a text and by which they run through a text, weaving their way from clause to clause and from sentence to sentence.

Theme dynamics must consist of three parts. The first part is a THEME STATICS, that is, a theory of theme in a clause and sentence. The second part must consist of a theory and method of THEMATIC IDENTIFICATION — some linguists might prefer to speak about IDENTIFICATION OF GIVEN — which enables us to compare thematically definable parts of different sentences and to decide whether we wish to regard them as the same or as different. And the third part should give a taxonomy for PATTERNS OF THEME MOVEMENT through the successive sentences of a text.

Approaches to theme statics are already available. Much less work has been done on theme dynamics (cf. DANEŠ 1970), though many of its problems have been touched upon in analyses of style and narrative structure (e.g. KOCH 1970). The basic problems of theme dynamics may therefore be worth illustrating here in terms of some examples deliberately restricted to written texts. In spoken ones, a number of complex features of stress, intonation and prosody would have to be reckoned with as well.

The second part of theme dynamics must, then, compare themes of different sentences and give methods of deciding whether two themes are the same or different, irrespective of whether they are expressed with the same words or not. At present, there is no sufficiently rigorous semantic theory of synonymy, and in practical stylistic analysis we must therefore content ourselves with some very rough-and-ready systems of theme identification. Themes may thus be regarded as the same if they fit into certain patterns of semantic relationship such as

repetition: The *process of charging* a capacitor consists of transferring a charge from the plate at lower potential to the plate at higher potential. The *charging process* therefore requires the expenditure of energy.

reference: On the station platform were *Negro soldiers. They* wore brown uniforms and were tall and *their* faces shone.

synonymy: *Rome* was still *the capital of the Pope.* As if she knew that her doom was upon her, *the Eternal City* arrayed herself to meet it in all her glory.

antonymy: *Wise men* should speak. *Fools* are much less interesting to listen to.

comparison: John was hurt by all these accusations. *Even more painful* were the suspicions of his wife.

contracting hyponymy: *People* got on and off. At the news-stand *Frenchmen*, returning to Paris, bought that day's papers.

expanding hyponymy: *Tulips* are cheap even in January. But then *flowers* seem to be necessary to Scandinavians during the darkest season.

co-membership of the same word field: *Tulips* are cheap. *Roses* are expensive.

sustained metaphor: The sun *sagged* yellow over the grass plots and *bruised itself* on the clotted cotton fields. The fertile countryside that grew things in other seasons spread flat from the roads and *lay prone* in ribbed fans of *broken* discouragement.

As even these few examples show, sentences are often thematically linked by the simultaneous use of more than one device of theme identification. In the example given above under "synonymy", the sentences were thus not only kept together by synonyms of Rome, but also by the reference *Rome — she — her — her*. If necessary, these categories can be further subdivided for greater delicacy. For instance in

> You could not get away from the *sun*. The only *shadows* were made by rocks.

the relationship between *sun* and *shadows* might be labelled with the semiotic term INDEXAL to indicate a special type of word-field relationship. And in passages like

> She had a strong sense of her own insignificance; of her life's slipping by while June bugs covered the moist fruit in the fig trees with the motionless activity of clustering flies upon an open sore. The bareness of the dry Bermuda grass about the pecan trees crawled imperceptibly with tawny caterpillars. The matlike vines dried in the autumn heat and hung

> like empty locust shells from the burned thickets about the
> pillars of the house.

it is hard to find simple instances of repetition, reference, or
synonymy, though the choice of words is homogeneous
enough. Here, one device holding the sentences together is
the repeated juxtaposition of botanical and zoological terms,
the way in which plants suggest insects and locust shells. Of
course such thematic looseness, such a lack of more stringently
definable patterns of reference, synonymy, and the like can be
a style marker in its own right.

Even if we succeed in thus developing a provisional apparatus for the identification of themes enabling us to trace
sets of themes through a text, we still need the third component of theme dynamics: the taxonomy of the ways in which
themes move through a text. To escape the difficulties of the
terms *theme* and *rheme*, which some, but not all, investigators
identify with *initial* and *non-initial sentence elements*, we
might strictly and operationally discuss thematic movement
in terms of two positions, I(nitial) and N(on-initial). If so,
we shall arrive at four possible patterns of thematic movement (assuming that I and N are precisely defined):

I to I: *The fields* outside the villages were full of vines. *The
   fields* were brown. (Identification device = repetition)
I to N: *A lady* stood in the midst of the hail of bullets. It
   was obviously impossible to frighten *her*. (Pronominal
   anaphoric reference)
N to I: The ratio of the velocity of light in a vacuum to the
   phase velocity of light of a particular wavelength in any
   substance is called *the index of refraction* of the substance
   for light of that particular wavelength. *The index of
   refraction* will be designated by *n*. (Repetition)
N to N: That afternoon Jack came to *London*. Peter was
   also *there*. (Anaphoric reference by adverbial of place)

If we have operationally unambiguous definitions for theme and rheme or topic and comment, we may of course substitute them for the distinction between I and N. Several other principles of classifying thematic movements could be devised. One criterion is syntactic function. Thus a theme may move from the subject of one sentence to the subject of another, from subject to object, from object to subject, and so on. Another is syntactic structure. Thematic features may thus move from noun phrase to verb phrase, from substantive to verb, and so forth. One principle of classification is based on the distance of sentences with related themes. Some texts make frequent use of thematic movements from one sentence to the next, that is, from sentence n to sentence $n + 1$, whereas in other texts, movements from sentence n to sentence $n + 2$, $n + 3$, and so on may be comparatively common.

A terminology for what I have here called *theme dynamics* was published by Frantisek DANEŠ after this chapter had been written (Daneš 1970a, 1970b). To identify themes, DANEŠ suggests the use of questions. If, for instance, we wish to find the theme in *Er bekam das Buch von einem Kollegen*, we should ask *Von wem bekam er das Buch?*, the answer, *Von einem Kollegen*, being the rheme, the rest — *Er bekam das Buch* — the theme. (Why we should not ask *Wer bekam das Buch von einem Kollegen?* or *Was bekam er von einem Kollegen?* is, however, not quite clear.) Further, DANEŠ classifies patterns of theme movement as

(a) simple linear progression, in which the rheme of one sentence becomes the theme of the next,
(b) passages with run-through themes (a sequence of sentences with the same theme but different rhemes),
(c) progression of derived themes (there is one *Hyperthema* and several hyponymic *Teilthemen*), and
(d) the development of a split rheme (the themes of successive

sentences are co-members of a concept forming the rheme of the initial sentence, as in

> Die Widerstandsfähigkeit [...] ist bei *verschiedenen Arten pathogener Viren* sehr unterschiedlich. *Poliomyelitisviren* sterben in trockene Luft sofort ab [...] Bei *Grippeviren* ist es hingegen umgekehrt [...]) (DANEŠ 1970b: 77).

Here, then, theme identification and theme movement have been fused into one single taxonomy. Such packaging of different features is no doubt practical in those analyses in which a group of co-occurring elements is likely to have stylistic significance. In actual practice, a complete consideration of all the factors of theme dynamics listed above will make the actual analysis of texts very slow and intricate. Indeed the work readily becomes so laborious that the processing of large bodies of text consumes time and energy beyond the point of diminishing returns. In theme-dynamic analysis as in all practical analyses of texts, the purpose must be allowed to determine the choice of levels of abstraction and delicacy. As long as stylistic analysis is viewed as a practical business, we shall do wisely in registering and counting only those features that are likely to function as style markers. The investigator will also very soon come to realize, and to learn the hard way, the need for simple methods of surveying and presenting his complex findings. One type of theme-dynamic display is the COHESION CHART, in which the clauses and sentences of a text are numbered and plotted against the various cohesion devices. Another is the STYLISTIC PROFILE, in which relative numbers of cohesion devices are given in staple diagrams or histograms.

Theme-dynamic patterns are not, however, the only means by which strings of sentences satisfy the requirements of textual well-formedness. In fact, textual well-formedness (or "TEXTUALITY") is a function of three major types of factors. First it depends on the grammatical well-formedness of the individual sentences. A text consisting of ill-formed sentences is ill-formed. Secondly, it depends on the way in which the sentences are strung together. And thirdly, as we noted above, it may also depend on the context: in a grammar-book we may tolerate a string of grammatical examples which make little or no sense outside their grammatical context.

In addition to anaphoric and cataphoric reference, pronominalization, the use of referential *do* or *one*, and other cohesion devices traditionally discussed in sentence grammar, there are yet other cohesion features that are amenable to linguistic analysis and description. Some of them may be readily listed:

CONTEXTUAL COHESION keeps together passages occurring in the same matrix of contextual features. For instance, a piece of dialogue in a novel has a contextual matrix different from a descriptive passage in the same novel; in a play, stage directions have a contextual matrix different from that of the dialogue; and so on. Sentences having the same contextual matrix are felt to belong together.

LEXICAL COHESION is a term suggesting that coherent texts often have a homogeneous vocabulary, which contributes to their unity. The homogeneity of the vocabulary may be affected by the subject matter of a text. An article on nuclear physics is likely to contain a high density of terms related to nuclear physics. It is also affected by other contextual features, including style: a colloquial text is likely to use a stylistically homogeneous, colloquial vocabulary.

CLAUSAL LINKAGE provides us with an arsenal of formal means marking the ways in which clauses cohere within sentences and sentences cohere within texts. Grammarians have traditionally paid attention to the ways in which clauses join into sentences, but though many of the devices of intersentence linkage are much the same as those of clausal linkage within the sentence, ways of linking sentences into texts still deserve special study (LONGACRE 1970). MILIC (1969: 21) has suggested a system of eight basically logical, rather than formal, relations between sentences. They are:

Additive, a proposition which has no organic relation with its predecessor (*and*).

Initial, the first sentence of a paragraph.

Adversative, a proposition which changes the direction of the argument (*but*).

Alternative, a proposition which may be substituted for the previous one (*or*).

Explanatory, a restatement, definition or expansion of the previous proposition (*that is*).

Illustrative, an instance or illustration (*for example*).

Illative, a conclusion (*therefore*).

Causal, the cause for a preceding conclusion (*for*).

Density patterns of types of sentence linkage may offer us a battery of additional style markers.

By ICONIC LINKAGE — another term borrowed from semiotics — I mean those situations in which two or more sentences cohere because they are, at some level of abstraction, isomorphic (or, more popularly, "pictures of each other"). For instance, one line of Pope is highly likely to be metrically isomorphic with another line of Pope. If so, these two lines cohere iconically at the metrical level. To use the term *iconic linkage* meaningfully, however, the investigator has to decide at what level of abstraction the isomorphism is significant as an iconic link. As a rule, such isomorphisms have to lie close to the surface: it would be meaningless in this connection to regard all sentences as pictures of each other merely because they all share some deep structure such as NP + VP. Instances of rhythmic and metrical regularities, rhyme, alliteration, and assonance all qualify as instances of iconic linkage. Iconic links may also be syntactic: they link *The old gentleman elegantly kissed the young lady* with *The striped tiger cruelly bit the innocent lamb*. They also connect CHOMSKY's classic examples *He is eager to please* and *He is easy to please, Revo-*

lutionary new inventions appear infrequently and *Colourless green ideas sleep furiously*. Such examples support the view that stylistically meaningful iconic links are based on similarities on, or close to, the surface.

There are yet other linguistic features that may add cohesion to a text, for instance the consistent use of certain tenses (WEINRICH 1964) or the consistent use of such aspects of point of view as can be linguistically defined (SINCLAIR 1968: 223–4). We are here approaching the border between text linguistics in the strict sense, and poetic or narrative analysis of the kinds developed by the Russian formalists, New Critics, and French Neo-Structuralists. Today, the wisest policy may well be to leave this border open and to welcome any translations of literary concepts and devices into linguistic terms. To mention just one instance: in some contexts, the first sentence of a text is marked by certain characteristics some of which are amenable to reasonably stringent linguistic description. This does not apply only to the *Once upon the time* of fairytales. In a body of scholarly articles in philological journals, there seems to be a restricted number of ways and means that writers use to provide their first sentences with apparent 'givens': existential thematization with *there is*, thematization with presuppositions expressed by *it is*, quotations, uses of what Sir George Rostrevor HAMILTON (1949) has called the "tell-tale article" (that is, uses of *the* in instances where the following noun is neither universally known nor given in a previous sentence), nominalizations (as in *The esteem in which scholars hold Bacon is* . . ., rather than *Scholars esteem Bacon*), general quantifiers such as *every* or *all*, and certain other structures seem to be particularly characteristic of text-initial sentences. Sometimes, too, writers use part of their title as 'given' and turn it into the theme of the first sentence. In a wider, less linguistic, description one might say that text-initial sentences reveal one of two possible strategies. Either the first sentence is frankly acknowledged as lacking a 'given' by the use of a narrative formula or existential phrase. Or the writer tries to hide this lack by appealing to undisputed facts, authorities, general statements, unquestioned nominalizations and the like, often marking them with the definite article to show that he assumes them to be known not only to himself but also to his reader. Beginning with a quotation is another way in which writers conjure forth a "PSEUDO-GIVEN".

What, then, is the significance of all these patterns of inter-sentence grammar and text linguistics for stylistic analysis?

First, they show what kinds of conceptual frames we must use if we agree that style is not merely a quality of sentences but also of texts. If so, we must also devise means of describing styles which reckon with textual, intersentential features and not only with terms that refer to phenomena within the confines of single sentences. The first step from a sentence stylistics to a text stylistics in this, more rigorous, sense where "text stylistics" is not merely the sum total of the stylistic analysis of individual sentences but also a consideration of the way in which sentences form texts, must be a close study of intersentence grammar. This must concern both spoken and written texts, for spoken language has its own ways of marking cohesion, theme, and forms. Here we are approaching text stylistics from the linguistic end. But text stylistics also has other aspects. For instance, the study of narrative patterns may be regarded as part of textual study. Here we are once again straining against the fence between stylolinguistics and literary stylistics. Some narrative patterns may be amenable to reasonably stringent, even linguistic, definition; others may not. Therefore the investigator who moves in this frontier area may find that some problems need a shift of method from linguistic to literary, or *vice versa*.

Secondly, patterns of intersentence grammar and text linguistics provide us with a vast arsenal of additional style markers. We may try to express the stylistic differential between text and norm with the aid of densities of cohesion devices. We may test hypotheses such as: "X's scientific style is characterized by a comparatively high density of thematic movements from rheme in sentence n to theme in sentence $n + 1$". Observations of textual cohesion patterns and of devices of theme dynamics may also yield materials for practical tasks such as the teaching of composition and of normative stylistics.

Altogether, LINGUISTIC TEXT STYLISTICS is an area which is gradually opening up for new types of inquiry. One possible rough classification of textual style markers is into three major fields: theme dynamics, including anaphoric and cataphoric reference; cohesion devices between sentences and larger textual units; and linkage which overtly marks relations between sentences.

STYLOSTATISTICS

Many linguists are likely to agree that style is affected by frequencies. In this book I have argued that the impression we have of the style of a text is caused by significant differences in the densities of linguistic features in this text, and in a norm consisting of another, contextually related text or body of text. In quantitative studies of such stylistic differentials, statistical methods may come to play an important rôle, not least in testing probable significance levels of the differences between text and norm.

In fact students of style have often made pseudo-quantitative statements of the type "N.N.'s style is characterized by the frequent use of construction x." Note that such statements in themselves imply comparison. If feature x is frequent in the style of N.N., and if this frequency is characteristic of N.N., it follows that others — and in fact those whose writings we regard as worth comparing with N.N.'s — use feature x less often than N.N. One possible source of disagreement lies in the choice of norm. If one critic finds N.N.'s use of feature x very frequent, and another finds N.N.'s use of the same feature very rare, both may still be right though they disagree. For as long as the norm remains undefined, one critic may have tacitly compared N.N. to A.A., the other to B.B. As soon as the text and the norm are explicitly defined, however, it becomes possible to move the discussion of such disagreements from the realms of opinion to the realms of verifiable fact. It becomes possible to set up inventories of

the stylistic differentials between text and norm, and it becomes possible to test their statistical significance. Of course
this need not end the disagreement and argument between
our two critics. One of them may still argue that the important and therefore significant comparison of N.N. should be
with A. A. and not with B.B., and perhaps also accuse his
opponent of having neglected to pay attention to those linguistic features that are really significant and therefore worth
counting. And the stylobehavioristic description of each
critic's responses to the same set of stimuli in a text will always remain subjective. Such subjectivity is the critic's
most precious privilege.

In the stylolinguistic description of texts, however, statistics has its given place. Style has often been viewed as a
statistical and probabilistic, not a deterministic, branch of
linguistics. In an earlier chapter, the capacity of making
statistical and probabilistic, and not only categorical, statements was regarded as one of the characteristics required of
those grammatical models that we wish to apply to stylolinguistic description. To those who see an opposition between a fundamentally deterministic linguistics and a fundamentally probabilistic stylistics, different methods are open
to resolve the conflict. One extreme solution would be to
divorce stylistics from linguistics. But as we have seen, neat
dichotomies between a deterministic *langue* and a probabilistic
parole have been opposed by those who find that certain
probabilities are likely to be inherent not only in texts but
also in our internalized linguistic rules. Another solution is
to build frequencies into one's theories of linguistics and
methods of language description.

8.2 SOME EARLY STYLOSTATISTICIANS. ZIPF AND YULE

In spite of frequent scepticism and many justifiable *caveats*
(e.g. POSNER 1963), the list of attempts to apply statistics to

the study of style is a long one. Those who wish to review statistical studies of language with style in mind will do wisely in noting that statisticians have in fact studied language with two very different aims. Some of them have tried to find those statistical patterns that are common to large samples of text, and perhaps even to all texts in all languages. They have, in other words, been looking for statistical universals. On the contrary, others have concentrated on extracting those features that make one text different from other texts. They have sought statistical differentials, not universals. For obvious reasons, students of style are primarily interested in the differential approach. They want to know how one text differs from another. But both approaches are nevertheless related and relevant. If we know what features can be regarded as statistical universals and thus as independent of the text and perhaps of the language, we may at once disregard them in our quest for stylistically significant statistical parameters. We may, in other words, set up an inventory of those statistical features that are potential style markers by subtracting the statistical universals from the total inventory of statistical characteristics of the text we are studying.

As long as we bypass early work such as the Massoretic studies of Biblical Hebrew, the writings of various kinds of linguistic numerologists, and the endeavours of cryptanalysts and other forerunners of linguistic statistics, the origins of stylostatistics can be found in the mid-nineteenth century. Augustus DE MORGAN, professor of mathematics in the University of London, showed his interest in the subject in a letter to the Reverend W. HEALD at Cambridge in 1851. He suggested that HEALD count word length in various Greek texts to prove

that one man writing on two different subjects agrees more closely with himself than two different men writing on the same subject. (WILLIAMS 1970: 5)

Such data could be used for author identification. A number
of critics gradually developed the STYLOMETRIC APPROACH to
literature. They studied both ancients and moderns by counting averages and percentages of lines with metrical variations,
rhyme, run-on lines, extra syllables and the like, though without those statistical controls of significance levels and standard
deviation that modern stylostatisticians regard as basic. One
important figure in this development was T. C. MENDENHALL,
an American physicist working in the last decades of the nine-
teenth century. He was apparently stimulated by a memoir
of DE MORGAN published by his widow in 1882; he studied a
number of texts — Dickens, Thackeray, John Stuart Mill,
Caesar, Shakespeare, Bacon, Marlowe, and others — in terms
of word-length distribution. One of the sophisticated features
of MENDENHALL's work was his reckoning with the influence
of sample size on the conclusions.

The importance of George Kingsley ZIPF (1902—1950) lies
in his having stimulated the statistical study of language,
especially its statistical universals. One of the focal points of
his interest was the relationship between word frequency and
word length: he found that in languages as different as Chinese,
Latin, and English, the length of words tends to have an
inverse relationship to their frequency. Common words are
shorter, rare words tend to be longer. Another of ZIPF's
contributions was an attempt at stating a massive, universal
relationship between WORD RANK and WORD FREQUENCY: if we
multiply the rank of a word (that is, its place on a frequency
list, so that the most frequent word has rank 1, the second
most frequent word rank 2, and so on) with its frequency, the
result is a constant. This relation holds best in the middle
region of the vocabulary, but is less accurate at both ends,
that is, with the most common words and with rare words.
ZIPF's critics have, however, suggested that the inverse relationship between rank and frequency is a statistical necessity
inherent in these two concepts, and not a characteristic of
language. ZIPF went on to speculate voluminously about the

all-important role of the principle of least effort in all human
behaviour, and about the character of language as a compro-
mise between elaboration and reduction, dull over-articulation
and incomprehensible under-articulation.

Very different in temperament was the Cambridge statistician, G. Udny YULE, whose achievement lies within differential rather than universal linguistic statistics. YULE had a close
look at "ZIPF's Law" but could not agree that it held a satisfactory degree of precision. One of his investigations concerned *De imitatione Christi* with the purpose of judging between
the claims of Thomas à Kempis and Jean Charlier de Gerson
as to its authorship. His main problem was to devise a
statistical measure relatively independent of sample size, and
for this purpose he developed a formula for "Yule's Characteristic". YULE's K can be regarded as a measure of the chance
that any two nouns selected at random in a given text will
be identical. YULE also used sentence length as a stylostatistical criterion.

Among those who have refined, and added to, the pioneering
studies of ZIPF and YULE, three theorists of linguistic statistics
should be briefly mentioned. Benoit MANDELBROT modified
ZIPF's rank-frequency formula by adding to it factors reflect-
ing certain features of individual texts. MANDELBROT's
formula gives better approximations than ZIPF's, though it
too has been criticised on the same grounds. Wilhelm FUCKS
studied particularly the number of syllables per word, not
only as a characteristic of various languages but also as a
feature of individual styles and of the diachronic development
of styles within a language. One of his additions was the concern with entropy which links stylostatistics with information
theory (see e.g. CHERRY 1957). And in numerous books and
articles, Gustav HERDAN presented a number of approaches
both to the study of linguistic universals and of stylistic
particulars, including many analyses of data both his own
and cited from other studies. HERDAN tried, among many
other things, to improve YULE's characteristic, and one of

his achievements is a stringent formulation of a vocabulary connectivity test measuring the lexical homogeneity between different partitions of a text or between different texts. Such tests give us chances of contrasting one portion of a text against a norm taken from the same text.

8.3 GUIRAUD. THEME WORDS AND KEY WORDS. JOSEPHINE MILES

In the works of Pierre GUIRAUD, we are introduced to the concepts of THEME WORDS, and KEY WORDS which are interesting both to stylolinguists and to content analysts. GUIRAUD begins by noting that in any text, a small number of words will make up the major part of the text: the 100 most frequent words account for 60 per cent, the 1,000 most frequent words for 85 per cent, and the 4,000 most frequent words for 97,5 percent of the text (GUIRAUD 1954). Having emphasized the importance of proper definitions of concepts such as 'word' — for definitions must be explicit and rigorous if we are to base statistical counts on them — GUIRAUD goes on to discuss characteristics of word distribution patterns in terms of rank *versus* frequency, and number *versus* frequency. One important type of calculation attempts computation of the size and structure of a writer's TOTAL LEXICON, of which the vocabulary actually appearing in a given text is a sample. With the aid of empirical data, GUIRAUD arrives at a way of estimating the total lexicon as a function of text length, the number of different words, and the structure of the vocabulary. He also sets up formulae for the calculation of measures for VOCABULARY CONCENTRATION, VOCABULARY DISPERSION, and VOCABULARY RICHNESS. The setting-up of norms for these functions will then permit comparison of individual texts with the norms. GUIRAUD's theme words, *mots-thèmes*, are those words that appear most frequently in a given writer's text (excluding function words). Key words, *mots-clés*, are those full words in the text whose frequencies significantly differ from their frequencies in the norm (GUIRAUD used VANDER BEKE's word-frequency list as the basis for the norm). The method permits conclusions such as that Rimbaud and Claudel have very much larger lexicons than Valéry, but that Rimbaud's vocabulary dispersion is greater and vocabulary concentration lower than Claudel's, so that Rimbaud can be said to put his large lexicon to fuller use.

Still more akin to content analysis are the studies of poetic vocabulary of Josephine MILES. Her materials consisted of 1,000 lines from each of 130 poets from different periods, and she focussed her series of investigations partly on high-frequency words and partly on proportions between adjectives, substantives, and verbs. The favourite words of poets and periods reflect on content, but MILES also defined certain major types of style in English poetry. One is a PHRASAL STYLE characterized by nominalizations and participles as well as by metrical irregularities. Another is a CLAUSAL STYLE marked by active use of verbs and a more complex sentence structure. And the third is a BALANCED, CLASSICAL STYLE which is intermediate between the first two. When matching the texts of different periods against these norms, each century from 1500 to 1900 is in fact found to fall into three parts, each of which is characterized by the dominance of one of the three stylistic norms.

8.4 APPROACHES AND STYLOSTATISTICAL CHARACTERISTICS

The student of style can thus easily find a number of studies that teach him the principles and methods of stylostatistics, partly in the works of the scholars mentioned above, partly in special textbooks (e.g. MULLER 1968) and anthologies (HALLBERG et alii. 1966, DOLEŽEL – BAILEY 1969). Statisticians cannot, however, tell students of style what features will be worth counting for stylistic significance. Statisticians operate with figures and take no responsibility for the correlations between the figures and the entities they stand for. The student of style must decide on his own what linguistic features he wishes to count in order to arrive at the figures that can be tested by statistical operations. In practice, no linguist can ever count all the features of a text of any length: even short texts include vast numbers of features and feature combinations that may be of stylistic significance. Therefore it is usually wise to begin by limiting the counting of features to those that the investigator suspects will support his observations and intuitions as to stylistic differentials between text and norm. Some hypotheses are reasonably safe: thus we may expect that the vocabulary patterns in the works of a given poet will contrast sufficiently against a general norm provided by a frequency dictionary to yield a set of what GUIRAUD called *key words*. Other hypotheses are not, and weeks of diligent counting may fail to produce significant results.

The distributions of sounds, phonemes, and letters appear to be language-bound and even to show certain universal distribution patterns. Therefore they are comparatively ill suited to the differentiation between one style and another, except in such areas as in metrics and in sound patterns where iconic relationships play a major role. FUCKS and some others have found that measures of word length such as the number of syllables per word can discriminate between individual styles and certain period styles within a given language. Most stylostatisticians have, however, worked at the lexical level. Here stylistic characteristics can be defined either in terms of general distributional characteristics of a text such as GUIRAUD's measures of richness, concentration, and dispersion, or in terms of frequencies of individual lexical items such as theme words and key words, or even certain function words. Proportions between native and borrowed words have also been used. At the syntactic level, sentence length and sentence complexity are among those features that are easiest to quantify, and they have therefore been another focus of statistical study. There are, so far, relatively few attempts at using intersentence patterns for stylostatistical purposes (SWIECZKOWSKI 1961, WINBURNE 1964).

8.5 SAMPLE AND NORM

Stylolinguistic criteria must, of course, always affect the decision whether one should embark on statistical analyses of one's materials or not. But the statistical operations themselves also place some limitations on stylostatistical studies. For instance, statistical formulae are apt to penalize those who use small samples. In some situations, a linguist cannot manipulate the sizes of his text and his norm; he may for instance be working with a dead language with few surviving texts, or with other kinds of closed texts. In other instances, the linguist can himself decide how large his samples are to be. If so, he may do wisely in consulting a statistician to find out what minimum texts he should analyse to get samples adequate for a statistical control of the significance of stylistic differentials. In addition to linguistic and to statistical factors, students of style must always reckon with the cost of labour and other economic realities. Elaborate analyses of large materials readily become impracticable because they involve vast amounts of text processing. In practice, nobody can count everything. The number of features one can count must in practice be limited to what the investigator can handle in his particular situation.

One way of saving labour is to use a norm which is already available and against which one's text can be matched. In many types of study, such ready-made norms do not exist. In other studies, a suitable hypothesis may make it possible to use already processed materials for norm. In word studies, for instance, we may define our norm as that large sample of language from different contexts that compilers of frequency dictionaries used for their frequency counts. For some studies,

such a norm may be too general; for others it may prove
adequate. Thus VANDER BEKE's word list was sufficient to
bring out the differences between the key words of several
French poets. Nowadays, large masses of text have been processed by compilers of frequency dictionaries, students of
usage, concordance-makers, and others; a student of style
with access to such materials may use them to great advantage,
for instance by extracting new information out of existing
data banks by means of computer programmes of his own.
There are many types of stylistic studies in which it would be
most unwise for the student to closet himself to count manually thousands or millions of features which might, with proper
permission and knowhow, be extracted from materials already
on tape for computer treatment. The periodical *Computers in
the Humanities* is one clearing-house of relevant information.

8.6 ATTRIBUTION STUDIES

It is one thing to start out from the observation that two
styles are different, and to apply statistics to check the
validity of this observation. It is another matter to apply
statistics to the testing of the hypotheses that two texts may,
or may not, be stylistically different. The statistical methods
used in both situations are, of course, very much the same.
But the latter type of question — testing whether text and
norm are significantly different or not — occurs in one particular variant of stylostatistics, namely author identification.
Attribution problems have, of course, been studied without
strict stylolinguistic quantification (ERDMAN – VOGEL 1966),
but they have gained in stringency with the introduction of
explicit statistical tests evaluating the probability levels at
which we may regard two texts as having been written by
the same person.

Once again, available statistical data on author identification support our definition of style as the aggregate of signi-

ficant differences between a text and a contextually related
norm. For what is done to identify the author of a text is a
comparison of the densities of selected linguistic features in
the problem text with the corresponding densities in a set of
comparable texts by the suspected author. In other words:
attribution studies are based on matching the densities in the
text with those in a norm, or in a set of norms. (Cf. HALLBERG
1962, 1963, 1968; McKINNON – WEBSTER 1969; MORTON 1965;
MUNDT 1969).

To exemplify these procedures, let us briefly glance at just
two of the best-known stylostatistical author attributions in
English. A classic instance is Alvar ELLEGÅRD's study of the
Junius Letters, the celebrated political pamphlets from the
eighteenth century whose authorship has been in dispute ever
since they burst upon the world. The letters themselves
comprise some 82,200 words. ELLEGÅRD matched them against
a norm comprising about one million words of political literature from the same period. His growing familiarity with this
genre suggested that some words were more common in the
Junius Letters than in the norm, and that others were less
common in the text than in the norm. ELLEGÅRD then went
on to count these "Junian plus" and "Junian minus" words.
As the likeliest identification of Junius was with Sir Philip
Francis, he also used a 231,300-word sample known to be by
Francis for an additional norm. The conclusions have to do
both with the authorship of the *Junius Letters* and with the
method. Sir Philip Francis indeed proved to be the most
likely author. As to method, ELLEGÅRD states that his
statistical test is sufficiently sensitive to identify the author
of a work, provided that the work itself amounts to 10,000
words or more (though considerable discrimination can be
obtained even with texts of 2,000 words), and that there is a
sample of about 100,000 words by the suspected author as
well as a comparable, contemporary sample of some 1,000,000
words of contextually related text. ELLEGÅRD's method also
included fusion of certain groups of features and texts with

the purpose of increasing their size and thus adding to the effectiveness of the test by minimizing the statistical penalization of small samples.

ELLEGÅRD's list contained 458 features, of which the majority were substantives, adjectives, verbs, and adverbs, and some were prepositional phrases, prepositions, and conjunctions. There are, however, situations where content words such as substantives, adjectives and verbs fail to discriminate between texts that may have been written by different authors. If no other criteria such as syntactic structures, sentence length, or word length can be used, the investigator is compelled to base his tests on densities of function words such as articles, conjunctions, pronouns, and auxiliary verbs. This was the method by which Frederick MOSTELLER and David L. WALLACE analysed the authorship of the disputed items in *The Federalist Papers* (MOSTELLER – WALLACE 1963, 1964; LEED 1966). By comparing the 18 papers known to be by Hamilton with the 14 papers certainly written by Madison, they set up a first list of 165 discriminator words, which was later reduced to those 30 words that had been found best to separate Hamilton's and Madison's works. Madison turned out to be the likelier author of the disputed papers. Apart from their statistical method which was based on Bayes's theorem and the Poisson distribution, the most interesting and surprising contribution of MOSTELLER and WALLACE to the methodology of stylostatistics was their demonstration of the discriminatory power of function words. These "utterly mundane high-frequency function words" such as *upon, also, and, by, of, on, there, this, to,* and *although* had often been dismissed as useless by students of author-identification techniques. It is in the nature of such words to appear in a wide spectrum of contexts, and it had therefore been assumed that their density pattern is relatively unaffected by style. But once they are shown to be capable of discriminating between different authors, as MOSTELLER and WALLACE did in their work, a study of their densities is in some respects very favourable in stylolinguistic investigations. To begin with, they are frequent; they are also less affected by content, genre, and subject matter than are many other types of linguistic features.

Stylistic tests and author-identification techniques have also been applied to forensic purposes, not only by scholars but also by others. Two of the cases freely publicized have been those of Bishop Helander in Sweden, whose career was ruined after a lawsuit centering on the authorship of a series of anonymous letters (three polemical publications are Modéer 1952, Runquist 1958, and Tenow 1963), and of Timothy John Evans in England, who was hanged in 1950 and posthumously pardoned in 1966 (Svartvik 1968). In the Helander case, the suspect was a highly literate professional man, and the comparison could be based on a number of books and articles he had written. The linguistic analysis of the Evans statements by Jan Svartvik had to be founded on slender materials consisting of policemen's written records of the oral statements of an illiterate. Though the materials fail to permit firm conclusions, those paragraphs that Evans later claimed were untrue and owed to his being frightened and upset proved to be linguistically somewhat different from those paragraphs which Evans persisted in admitting as true evidence. Even the Helander case was, of course, not decided on the strength of linguistic evidence alone. Opinions differ as to what weight stylostatistics and author identification can, and should, carry as judicial evidence. Even those who believe that a person's style is one of his stable individual characteristics must reckon with the possibility of stylistic imitation and forgery. It is another matter that stylostatistics may, under suitable circumstances, claim considerable discriminating power. Thus chi-square testing of 19 stylistic variables in samples of 1,000 words sufficed to distinguish adequately between 19 Greek and Roman writers (Moerk 1970). Such findings should not, however, be rashly translated into forensic terms.

8.7 SUMMARY

Altogether, stylostatistics is capable of two types of operation. It can devise statistical parameters of various kinds, such as those listed by GUIRAUD, HERDAN, and MISTRIK (1967). And it can test the fit and significance level of various hypotheses and data, and thus estimate the likelihood that certain differences and distribution patterns owe to choice and not to chance. Any textbook on statistics will contain relevant information on these approaches to the testing of significance. They range from simple standard-deviation and chi-square analysis to very elaborate and sophisticated devices.

8.8 THE ROLE OF THE COMPUTER

Before we leave stylostatistics, a glance at the role of the computer in studies of language is in order. In fact it already entered into our argument in section *8.5.2*. In processing large masses of text, the computer is often useful, and sometimes an indispensable aid: there are certain types of investigation that cannot in practice be carried out without computer assistance. Some of these investigations involve too much mechanical drudgery, others too much meticulous precision, for any investigator, assistant, or team working manually. Still, as any investigator will very quickly find, computer studies cannot be undertaken lightly. First, the problems have to be defined with very great precision. Often a student of style is groping in a jungle of hypotheses too vague for exact programming. Then there are the costs of programming, input (card or tape punching), and actual computer time. Once the problem has been given a formulation sufficiently exact for programming, the decision becomes largely economic — not a problem of what can be done, but one of what is worth doing. If the text is already available in punched format or on tape — either in a text bank or, as in Sture ALLÉN's frequency dictionaries, on tapes used for the typesetting of newspapers — one major expense, that of input, has been eliminated.

What, then, can the computer do? The basic operations are few in number. A computer can sort out large numbers of items and thus produce suitably ordered lists such as concordances or, in reverse, rhyme indices. If the input consists of coded representations, for instance of syntactic structures, the computer can sort out these in any desired order by any criterion or combination of criteria. The computer can also count the items it lists. And it can perform any numerical calculations, for instance of all those controls of significance that enter into stylostatistics. Out of combinations of simple operations, we may build very complex programmes for specific purposes. Computers can collate texts, list collocations and co-occurrences of features, list those sentences out of different texts that share certain features or feature combinations, and the like. (Examples are available in BESSINGER 1964, LEED 1966, BOWLES 1967, and ALLÉN – THAVENIUS 1970.) But even if the computer can perform the desired operations, the crucial question for the investigator is likely to be economical. Are the yields likely to stand in a reasonable relation to the expense? In practice, manual pilot studies simulating computer operations as well as preruns of limited materials will often save the investigator from costly mistakes. So far, relatively few linguists have fully mastered the intricacies of programming and computer technology and been able to keep their knowledge and skill up to date. Therefore most students of style who wish to embark on computer studies will have to find and to employ programmers willing to immerse themselves in the special problems of the stylolinguistic processing of texts.

Quite a few aids for the study of styles have already been produced with the aid of computers. The number of COMPUTER CONCORDANCES is steadily increasing. Students of English are by now familiar with the Cornell concordances of Matthew Arnold, Blake, Emily Dickinson, and Yeats. Marvin

SPEVACK's Shakespeare concordance (SPEVACK 1968–70) is the best example so far of a CONTEXT-SENSITIVE WORD LIST. In fact SPEVACK's concordance is not one but several, inter-locking concordances: one for each character, one for each play, one for each group of plays, and one for the whole of Shakespeare. Such contextual partition makes possible a rapid matching of a large number of Shakespearean subtexts against any other Shakespearean subtext or combination of subtexts. We may, for instance, rapidly analyse the individual vocabularies of Shakespeare's characters and match them against the vocabularies of other characters or character groups. Another advantage of computer concordances for the student of style is their ease of giving full lists of gram-matical form-words. They can be stylistically significant, but were often omitted from manually compiled concordances because of the labour involved.

Another category of aid nowadays provided by computer is the FREQUENCY DICTIONARY. (JOSSELSON 1953, JELINEK – BEČKA – TEŠITELOVA 1961, ŠTEJNFEL'DT 1963, JUILLAND – CHANG-RODRIGUEZ 1964, JUILLAND – EDWARDS – JUILLAND 1965, KUČERA – FRANCIS 1967, MISTRIK 1969, ALLÉN 1971). As noted above, the very general character of such overall frequency dictionaries may make their use awkward for those stylistic purposes in which we need a contextually more re-stricted norm. Some frequency dictionaries do, however, offer data on contextually restricted subsections of the corpus. And even the general lists can be used for the basis of indirect com-parisons. Thus if we wish to compare a text T with a norm N, we may try to compare both, T and N, separately with the frequency dictionary, and then base our comparison of T and N on the results of the two differentials, that between T and the frequency dictionary and that between N and the fre-quency dictionary. Such comparisons will give us a measure of the similarities and differences between T and N in the light of a large, contextually more varied sample of language. Of course the older, manually compiled frequency dictionaries

(KAEDING 1898, MEIER 1967, VANDER BEKE 1929, THORN-
DIKE–LORGE 1944, etc.) are still useful, too. And special word
lists such as those of the *Enquête du français élémentaire* of St.
Cloud (GOUGENHEIM 1959) and the Finnish dictionary of school-
children's vocabularies (KARVONEN *et alii* 1970) have a more
direct concern with contextually restricted styles.

In addition to computer programmes devised for content
analysts but also applicable to work with style (STONE *et alii*
1966), there are descriptions of computer programmes designed especially for stylistic analysis. Thus Sally A. SEDELOW's
VIA programme is essentially a thesaurus establishing collocations for stylistic comparison, her MAPTEXT being a code
adaptable to the study of syntagmatic patterns of various
kinds (SEDELOW 1965–67, 1966).

8.9 PERSPECTIVES

Stylostatistics, then, is an area where different cultures meet.
In some quarters there has been a curious reluctance to admit
statistics, and particularly computer-produced ones, into
linguistic and literary study. There is a fear of technology in
general and the statistical trivialization of the humanities in
particular. Indeed it is true that the computer now makes it
possible for us to produce enormous quantities of meaningless
figures more rapidly than ever before. At the same time, it
gives us a chance of obtaining meaningful data that used to
be denied us by the mechanical labour involved in their extraction. The responsibility, the praise or the blame, should
not, however, be placed on the computers but on the
men and women who use them. A computer only obeys
orders; the scholars and students are the ones who ought to
guarantee that its capacities are not misused and that the
statistical figures represent meaningful data. Those who still
fear that the humanities will be inundated by vast masses of
computer-produced statistics, containing plenty of sound and

fury but signifying nothing, can also seek comfort in the fact that computerized research is neither cheap nor particularly convenient or soothing to the investigator. In practice, considerations of economy and of personal convenience will often combine to keep investigators from using computers until they really must.

9

CONCLUSION AND SUMMARY

In this book, style has been viewed as one of the responses that people have to texts. Irrespective of how they try to verbalize their impressions of this response, the response itself is based on the tacit or explicit comparison of the text with an imagined or explicit norm which the recipient regards as a relevant background for the text. The norm against which the text is matched is chosen on the basis of contextual relevance, context being definable as the aggregate of stylistically relevant features in the textual and situational envelopes surrounding the text. Our impressions of styles result from comparisons of densities of linguistic features in the text and in the contextually related norm: features common in their context give a different impression from features that are rare in that context. The choice of norm is, however, dependent on the recipient. Different people may compare the same text with different norms and may accordingly view the style of that text in a different light. The comparison of text and norm will result in observations of similarities as well as of differences.

From a point of view starting from the generation of texts, stylistically significant linguistic features have also been viewed as results of stylistic choice. However, the range of choice available to the speaker/writer does not appear from the text itself. If style is to be analysed in terms of choice, we must, first of all, be capable of distinguishing stylistic choice from other types such as pragmatic and grammatical choice. Secondly, we shall need a linguistic apparatus which explicitly maps out all those alternatives from among which the one actually present in the text was chosen. In the past fifteen years, linguistic models have become much more explicit in their description of the sequence of choices that lead to the generation of a given sentence. No model presently available is, however, capable of offering detailed mechanisms showing precisely how a generative grammar could react to matrices of contextual features and choose stylistic variants appropriate to each situation.

When we hear or read a text in its linear, temporal progression, we analyse it simultaneously in a number of ways. One of these analyses takes place in terms of stylistic probabilities. These probabilities are determined by the context and by our past experience of the densities of linguistic features in contexts that we regard as comparable. Our past experience of contextual frequencies thus turns into a set of present probabilities, against which we match the features that actually emerge during the progression of the text. In certain societies, epochs, and styles, high conformity to contextual probabilities has been at a premium. Individual departures from the norm have been frowned upon; surprises are regarded as undesirable, ugly, vulgar, socially dangerous, or even morally reprehensible. In other societies, epochs, and genres, communicants have been praised for their novel departures from stylistic norms. That poet has been said to be the greatest who has most departed from the language customarily used in the same kind of poetry. Thus some periods favour a classic harmony, others a romantic disorder; some groups have been conditioned to love fulfilled expectations, whereas others have preferred the shocks of surprise.

Those linguistic features whose densities in the text are significantly different from those in the norm are called *style markers*. Style markers are not absolutes: their inventory depends not only on the text but also on the choice of norm. If the norm changes, the inventory of style markers may also change. Style markers may be features whose frequency in the text is greater or smaller than in the norm. Thus the absence of features that are usually present in similar contexts can be a style marker, too.

Any linguistic features may function as style markers. Some may be paralinguistic and include an individual's voice or gestures. Others may be phonetic: in English, they might involve greater or less use of "weak" or "reduced" forms in solemn contexts. Rhythmic patterns, including *cursus*, may mark both poetic and prose styles. Examples of morphological style markers would be the use of *thou lovest* and *he loveth* in English, and *I ären* in Swedish, religious texts. Some style markers are lexical, as in *nice chap* and *fine man;* others are syntactic and may comprise not only individual syntactic features within clauses and sentences, but also word order and sentence complexity and length. Nor do style markers stop at the borders of sentences. Intersentence cohesion devices, patterns of theme dynamics, ways of opening texts or sections of text, and other features of intersentence grammar and text linguistics will provide us with a large stock of additional style markers. Orthographic and typographical devices of different types may also help to mark written styles. And as new areas of language become accessible to stringent linguistic description, we shall gain new potential style markers which are today counted among rhetorical and literary, not linguistic, features.

As my attempts at definitions have shown, style is a notational term, an abbreviation for a concept that can be defined in terms of other, more basic, concepts. Style is not a linguistic prime. This means that each stylolinguist owes to his readers an explicit report of precisely what he means by *style*, and by what methods he has arrived at his results and conclusions. The virtue of linguistic stylistics, as opposed to other kinds of stylistics, rests squarely on its ability to make precise, objectively verifiable statements.

Linguistic stylistics applies certain linguistic concepts to the study of texts. But the same texts will most likely be worth studying from other points of view and with other methods as well. Of all people, students of style ought to be least parochial: they work in a busy border zone, where courtesy and tact should count as virtues. When the methods of stylolinguistics prove inadequate, the needs of textual analysis may in fact suggest borrowing from neighbouring areas such as rhetoric and literary study. There is also another branch of linguistic stylistics, that trying to provide for stylistic variation in linguistic theory. Here, different linguistic theories must be evaluated on the basis of their capacity to include styles, and developed so that they can better incorporate varieties of language such as styles.

A number of studies of linguistic stylistics begin by stating that stylolinguistics has come of age, and I feel bound to repeat this true, though perhaps commonplace, statement as my final remark. The surge of interest was marked by events such as the Bloomington conference in 1958 and the stylolinguistic debate in *Voprosy Jazykoznanija* in the middle 'fifties. Those wishing to substantiate the continuous and growing preoccupation with style may count articles on stylistic subjects in linguistic journals, list new periodicals devoted largely or entirely to stylistic questions, and cite the development of sections on stylistics at linguistic congresses in support of their views. Also, thanks to an increasingly lively debate, a number of fundamental questions of stylolinguistics have been brought out to the fore and given their due perspective. On some of them, there is increasing agreement. Many others remain unsolved. Some will be solved differently by different schools of linguists. And many answers are bound to change with the changes and developments in linguistic perspectives. A number of different movements and specialities have already arisen within linguistic stylistics, and many more are bound to come. Different areas of specialization exist, and no single person can hope to master, or even follow, all the lines of development that are topical today. If an introduction of the size of mine succeeds in giving its readers some of the basic perspectives they need for further reading, it has achieved its goal.

10

BIBLIOGRAPHY

A very large number of articles bearing on stylistics and on styles has been, and is being, published in a very wide range of linguistic and literary periodicals, some of which — such as *Language and Style, Lingua e stile*, and *Style* — are expressly devoted to stylistics. Standard bibliographies such as the *Bibliographie linguistique, Language and Language Behavior Abstracts (LLBA)*, the annual bibliography of the Modern Language Association of America, the *Annual Bibliography of English Studies*, the *Year's Work in English Studies*, and the *Year's Work in Modern Language Studies*, as well as more specialized bibliographies contain numerous references to relevant books and articles. Many of the literary and period bibliographies often scatter relevant references and therefore need close perusal.

10.1 STYLISTIC BIBLIOGRAPHIES

Bailey, Richard W. – Dolores M. Burton
  1968 *English Stylistics; a Bibliography* (Cambridge, Mass. — London: The M.I.T. Press).
Bailey, Richard – Lubomir Doležel
  1968 *An Annotated Bibliography of Statistical Stylistics* (= *Michigan Slavic Series*) (Ann Arbor, Mich.: University of Michigan Press).
Guiraud, Pierre
  1954 *Bibliographie critique de la statistique linguistique* (Utrecht — Anvers: Spectrum Publishers).
Hatzfeld, Helmut
  1952 *A Critical Bibliography of the New Stylistics Applied to the Romance Literatures, 1900—1952 (= University of North*

Carolina Studies in Comparative Literature 5) (Chapel Hill, N.C.: University of Carolina).

1955 *Bibliografía crítica de la nueva estilística applicada a las literaturas románicas* (Madrid: Gredos).

Hatzfeld, Helmut – Yves Le Hir
1961 *Essai de bibliographie critique de stylistique française et romane (1955—1960)* (Paris: Presses Universitaires de France).

Milic, Louis T.
1967 *Style and Stylistics; an Analytical Bibliography* (New York: The Free Press).

Todorov, Tzvetan
1970 "Les Études du style; bibliographie sélective", *Poétique* 2: 224–32.

Tyl, Zdeněk (ed.)
1970 *A Tentative Bibliography of Studies in Functional Sentence Perspective* (Praha: Československa Akademie Ved).

Many of the books and articles listed below contain extensive bibliographies.

10.2 BOOKS AND ARTICLES

The following list contains the items referred to in the text, as well as a small selection of other representative works. Many important older studies have been omitted because references to them are available in the works listed here. Collections of papers have been marked with c, and only those articles that are expressly referred to in the text have been re-listed separately under their authors' names.

Adamec, P.
1966 *Porjadok slov v sovremennom russkom jazyke* [Word order in contemporary Russian] *(= Rozpravy ČSAV – RSP* 76.15) (Praha: Československa Akademie Věd).

Admoni, V. G.
1966 "Razmer predloženija i slovosočetanija kak javlenie sintaksičeskogo stroja" [Length of sentences and of word combinations as phenomena of syntactic structure], *Voprosy jazykoznanija* 15.4: 111–8.

Akhmanova, O.S. *et alii*
c1963 *Exact Methods in Linguistic Research*, translated from the

Russian by David G. Hays and Dolores V. Mohr (Berkeley – Los Angeles: University of California Press).

c1966 *O principax i metodax lingvostilističeskogo issledovanija* [On principles and methods of linguostylistic research] (Moskva: Izdatel'stvo Moskovskogo Universiteta).

Åkermalm, Åke
1965 *Rubriksvenska* [The Swedish of headlines] *(= Skrifter utgivna av Modersmålslärarnas förening* 100) (Lund: Gleerups).

Allén, Sture
1970a *Nusvensk frekvensordbok* 1 (Göteborg: Almqvist & Wiksell).
1970b "Vocabulary Data Processing" in BENEDIKTSSON (1970: 235–61).

Allén, Sture – Jan Thavenius (eds.)
c1970 *Språklig databehandling. Datamaskinen i språk- och litteraturforskning* [Language data processing. The computer in linguistic and literary research] (Lund: Studentlitteratur).

Alonso, Amado
1942 "The Stylistic Interpretation of Literary Texts", *Modern Language Notes* 57: 489–96.

Anttila, Raimo
1963 "Loanwords and Statistical Measures of Style in the *Towneley Plays*", *Statistical Methods in Linguistics* 2: 73–93.

Austin, J. L.
1962 *How to Do Things with Words* (Oxford: The Clarendon Press).

Bach, Emmon – Robert T. Harms (eds.)
c1968 *Universals in Linguistic Theory* (New York, etc.: Holt, Rinehart and Winston, Inc.).

Bally, Charles
1951 *Traité de stylistique française*[3], 2 vol. (Geneva: Georg; Paris: Klincksieck).

Barthes, Roland
1966 *Le Degré zéro de l'écriture* (Paris: Éditions du Seuil).

Barthes, Roland (ed.)
c1966 *L'Analyse structurale du récit* (= *Communications* 8) (Paris: Éditions du Seuil).

Benediktsson, Hreinn (ed.)
c1970 *The Nordic Languages and Modern Linguistics*; Proceedings of the International Conference of Nordic and General Linguistics, University of Iceland, Reykjavik, July 6–11, 1969 (Reykjavik: Visindafélag islendinga).

Beneš, Eduard
1968 "On Two Aspects of Functional Sentence Perspective", *Travaux Linguistiques de Prague* 3: 267–74.

Bense, Max

1962　*Theorie der Texte; eine Einführung in neuere Auffassungen und Methoden* (Köln: Kiepenheuer & Witsch).

1969　*Einführung in die informationstheoretische Ästhetik; Grundlegung und Anwendung in der Texttheorie* (Reinbek–Hamburg: Rowohlt).

Bezzel, Chris

1969　"A Grammar of Modern German Poetry", *Foundations of Language* 5: 470–87.

Bickerton, Derek

1969　"Prolegomena to a Linguistic Theory of Metaphor", *Foundations of Language* 5: 34–52.

Bessinger, Jess B., Jr., *et alii*

c1964　*IBM Literary Data Processing Conference Proceedings* (New York: Modern Language Association, Materials Center).

Birdwhistell, Ray L.

1952　*Introduction to Kinesics; an Annotation System for Analysis of Body Motion and Gesture* (Washington, D. C.: Department of State Foreign Service Institute).

Bloomfield, Leonard

1933　*Language* (New York: Henry Holt Company).

Bloomfield, Morton

1967　"The Syncategorematic in Poetry: From Semantics to Syntactics", in: *To Honor Roman Jakobson; essays on the Occasion of His Seventieth Birthday 11 October 1966 (= Janua Linguarum, series maior* 31) (The Hague – Paris: Mouton), pp. 309–17.

Boost, Karl

1959　*Neue Untersuchungen zum Wesen und zur Struktur des deutschen Satzes; der Satz als Spannungsfeld (= Deutsche Akademie der Wissenschaften zu Berlin, Veröffentlichungen des Instituts für deutsche Sprache und Literatur* 4) (Berlin: Akademie-Verlag).

Bloch, Bernard

1953　"Linguistic Structure and Linguistic Analyses", in: *Report of the Fourth Annual Round Table Meeting on Linguistics and Language Teaching* (Ed.: Archibald A. Hill) (= *Monograph Series on Language and Linguistics* 4) (Washington, D. C.: Georgetown University Press), pp. 40–4.

Bowles, E. A. (ed.)

c1967　*Computers in Humanistic Research* (Englewood Cliffs, N. J.: Prentice-Hall Inc.)

Bowman, Elizabeth
1966   *The Minor and Fragmentary Sentences of a Corpus of Spoken English (=Publications of the Indiana University Research Center in Anthropology, Folklore, and Linguistics* 42) (The Hague: Mouton).

Brewster, William T. (ed.)
1913a   *English Composition and Style; a Handbook for College Students* (New York: The Macmillan Company).
c1913b   *Representative Essays on the Theory of Style* (New York: The Macmillan Company).

Brook, G. L.
1970   *The Language of Charles Dickens* (London: André Deutsch).

Brooke-Rose, Christine
1958   *A Grammar of Metaphor* (London: Secker and Warburg).

Brown, Huntington
1966   *Prose Styles; five Primary Types (= Minnesota Monographs in the Humanities* 1) (Minneapolis, Minn.: University of Minnesota Press).

Buttke, Kurt
1963   "Besonderheiten der Wortfolge in Stilen der russischen Literatursprache der Gegenwart", *Zeitschrift für Slawistik* 8: 785–92.
1969   *Gesetzmässigkeiten der Wortfolge im Russischen (= Linguistische Studien)* (Halle/Saale: Max Niemeyer Verlag).

Budagov, R. A.
1967   *Literaturnye jazyki i jazykovye stili* [Literary languages and language styles] *(= Biblioteka filologa)* (Moskva: Vysšaja škola).

Caplan, Harry (ed.)
1954   [*Cicero*] *ad C. Herennium De ratione dicendi – Rhetorica ad Herennium (=Loeb Classical Library)* (London: William Heinemann Ltd.; Cambridge, Mass.: Harvard University Press).

Carvell, H. T. – Jan Svartvik.
1969   *Computational Experiments in Grammatical Classification (= Janua Linguarum, series minor* 61) (The Hague: Mouton).

Cassirer, Peter
1970   *Deskriptiv stilistik; en begrepps- och metoddiskussion* [Descriptive stylistics; a discussion of concepts and methods] *(= Acta Universitatis Gothoburgensis, Nordistica Gothoburgensia* 4) (Stockholm: Almqvist and Wiksell).

Catford, I. C.
 1965 *A Linguistic Theory of Translation* (= *Language and Language Learning* 8) (London: Oxford University Press).
Chapman, R. A.
 1967 *The Interpretation of Deviant Sentences*, Dissertation, University of California, Berkeley. (Ann. Arbor, Mich.: University Microfilms No. 68–5702).
Chatman, Seymour
 1962 "Linguistic Style, Literary Style and Performance: Some Distinctions", *Georgetown Monographs on Language and Linguistics* 13: 73–81.
 1966 "On the Theory of Literary Style", *Linguistics* 27: 13–25.
 1967 "Style: A Narrow View", *College Composition and Communication* 18: 72–6.
 1969 "New Ways of Analyzing Narrative Structure, with an Example from Joyce's *Dubliners*", *Language and Style* 2: 3–36.
Chatman, Seymour (ed.)
 c1971 *Literary Style: A Symposium* (New York: Oxford University Press).
Chatman, Seymour – Samuel R. Levin (eds.)
 c1967 *Essays on the Language of Literature* (Boston: The Houghton Mifflin Company).
Cherry, Colin
 1966 *On Human Communication*² (Cambridge, Mass. – London: The M. I. T. Press).
Chisholm, William S., Jr.
 1967 "An Exercise in Syntactic Stylistics", *Linguistics* 33: 24–36.
Chomsky, Noam
 1957 *Syntactic Structures* (= *Janua Linguarum, series minor* 4) (The Hague: Mouton).
 1965 *Aspects of the Theory of Syntax* (Cambridge, Mass.: M. I. T. Press).
 1966 "Topics in the Theory of Generative Grammar", in: *Current Trends in Linguistics* (Ed.: Thomas A. Sebeok) 3 (The Hague, – Paris: Mouton).
Christiansen, Broder
 1909 *Philosophie der Kunst* (Hanau: Clauss & Feddersen).
Closs, see Traugott
Cooper, Lane (ed.)
 c1907 *Theories of Style* (New York: The Macmillan Company).
Coseriu, Eugenio
 1962 *Teoría del lenguaje y lingüística general* (Madrid: Gredos).

Craddock, Sister Clare Eileen
  1952 *Style Theories as Found in Stylistic Studies of Romance Scholars (1900—1950)* (= *Catholic University of America, Studies in Romance Languages and Literatures* 43) (Cambridge: University Microfilms). [typescript]
Cressot, Maurice
  1947 *Le style et ses techniques* (Paris: Presses Universitaires de France).
Croce, Benedetto
  1904 *Estetica como scienza dell'espressione e linguistica generale*[2] (Palermo: Sandron).
Croll, Morris W.
  1966 *Style, Rhetoric and Rhythm;* essays by Morris W. Croll edited by J. Max Patrick, Robert O. Evans *et alii* (Princeton, N. J.: Princeton University Press).
Crosland, M. P.
  1962 *Historical Studies in the Language of Chemistry* (London, etc.: Heinemann).
Crystal, David – Randolph Quirk
  1964 *Systems of Prosodic and Paralinguistic Features in English* (= *Janua Linguarum, series minor* 39) (The Hague: Mouton).
Crystal, David – Derek Davy
  1969 *Investigating English Style* (London — Harlow: Longmans, Green and Co. Ltd.).
Cunningham, J. V. (ed.)
  1966 *The Problem of Style* (Greenwich, Conn.: Fawcett WorldLibrary).
Dahl, Liisa
  1970 *Linguistic Features of the Stream-of-Consciousness Techniques of James Joyce, Virginia Woolf and Eugene O'Neill* (= *Annales Universitatis Turkuensis* B. 116) (Turku: Turun Yliopisto).
Dahl, Östen
  1969 *Topic and Comment; a Study in Russian and General Transformational Grammar* (= *Acta Universitatis Gothoburgensis, Slavica Gothoburgensia* 4) (Stockholm: Almquist & Wiksell).
Daneš, František
  1964 "A Three-Level Approach to Syntax", *Travaux linguistiques de Prague* 1: 225–40.
  1970a "One Instance of Prague School Methodology: Functional Analysis of Utterance and Text", in: *Method and Theory in Linguistics* (Ed.: Paul L. Garvin) (= *Janua Linguarum, series maior* 40) (The Hague – Paris: Mouton).
  1970b "Zur linguistischen Analyse der Textstruktur", *Folia Linguistica* 4: 72–8.

Danks, Joseph H.
  1969 "Grammaticalness and Meaningfulness in the Comprehension of Sentences", *Journal of Verbal Learning and Verbal Behavior* 8: 687–96.
Davie, Donald
  1952 *Purity of Diction in English Verse* (London: Chatto & Windus).
  1955 *Articulate Energy* (London: Routledge – Kegan Paul).
  1963 *The Language of Science and the Language of Literature, 1700–1740 (= Newman History and Philosophy of Science Series* 13) (London – New York: Sheed – Ward).
Delbouille, P.
  1960 "Définition du fait de style", *Cahiers d'analyse textuelle* 2: 94–104.
Denison, Norman
  1969 "Sociolinguistics and Plurilingualism" in GRAUR (1970 1: 551–9).
DeVito, Joseph A.
  1967 "Style and Stylistics; an Attempt at Definition", *Quarterly Journal of Speech* 53: 248–55.
Devoto, Giacomo
  1950 *Studi di stilistica* (Firenze: Le Monnier).
  1962 *Nuovi studi di stilistica (= Biblioteca di litteratura e dell'arte)* (Firenze: Le Monnier).
  1969 "Criticism of Style in Italy", *Style* 3: 17–26.
Dijk, T. A. van
  1970a "Nogle aspekter af en generativ-transformationel tekstteori" [Some aspects of a generative transformational text theory], *Poetik* 3: 155–77.
  1970b "Sémantique générative et théorie des textes", *Linguistics* 62: 66–95.
Doležel, Lubomir
  1960 *O stylu moderni ceské prózy* [On the style of modern Czech prose] (Praha: Československa Akademie Ved).
  1967 "The Prague School and the Statistical Theory of Poetic Language," *Prague Studies in Mathematical Linguistics* 2: 97–104.
Doležel, Lubomir – Richard W. Bailey (eds.)
  c1969 *Statistics and Style* (New York: American Elsevier Publishing Company Inc.).
Doležel, Lubomir – Karel Hausenblas
  1961 "O sootnošenii poetiki i stilistiki" [On the interaction of poetics and stylistics], in: *Poetics. Poetyka. Poètika* 1 (Eds.:

D. Davie, I. Fonagy, R. Jakobson *et alii*) (Warszawa: Pan-stwowe Wydawnictwo Naukowe; 's-Gravenhage: Mouton & Co.), pp. 39–52.

Drijkoningen, F. F. J.

1963 "Stilistiek en het Onderzoek der Periodestijlen" [Stylistics and the investigation of period styles], *Forum der Letteren* 4: 207–14.

Dubois, J. *et alii*

1970 *Rhétorique générale* (= *Langue et langage*) (Paris: Librairie Larousse).

Einarsson, Jan

1971 *Sammanträdet som talsituation* (= *Lundastudier i nordisk språkvetenskap* C.4) (Lund: Studentlitteratur).

Ellegård, Alvar

1962a *A Statistical Method for Determining Authorship; the Junius Letters, 1769–1771* (= *Gothenburg Studies in English* 13) (Göteborg: Elanders Boktryckeri Aktiebolag).

1962b *Who Was Junius?* (Stockholm etc.: Almqvist – Wiksell).

Ellis, Jeffrey

1966 "On Contextual Meaning", in: *In Memory of J. R. Firth* (Ed.: C. E. Bazell *et alii*) (London: Longmans), pp. 79–95.

Ellis, Jeffrey – Jean N. Ure

1968 "Language Varieties, Register" in MEETHAM – HUDSON (1969: 251–9).

Enkvist, Nils Erik

1969 "Stylistics in Sweden and Finland; a Historical Survey", *Style* 3: 27–43.

1971 "On the Place of Style in Some Linguistic Theories" in CHATMAN (1971).

Enkvist, Nils Erik – John Spencer – Michael Gregory

1964 *Linguistics and Style* (= *Language and Language Learning* 6) (London: Oxford University Press).

Erdman, David V. – Ephim G. Vogel (eds.)

c1966 *Evidence for Authorship; Essays on Problems of Attribution* (Ithaca, N. Y.: Cornell University Press).

Erlich, Viktor

1969 *Russian Formalism; history — Doctrine* (= *Slavic Printings and Reprintings* 4) (The Hague: Mouton).

Faccani, Remo – Umberto Eco (eds.)

c1969 *I sistemi di segni e lo strutturalismo Sovietico* (Milano: Valentino Bompiani).

Fasold, Ralph W.

1970 "Two Models of Socially Significant Linguistic Variation", *Language* 46: 551–63.

158   BIBLIOGRAPHY

Ferguson, Charles A.
    1964   "Diglossia" in HYMES (1964: 429–39).
Fillmore, Charles J.
    1969   "Types of Lexical Information" in KIEFER (1969: 109–37).
Firbas, Jan
    1964a "From Comparative Word-Order Studies", *Brno Studies in
           English* 4: 111–28.
    1964b "On Defining the Theme in Functional Sentence Analysis",
           Travaux linguistiques de Prague 1: 267–80.

    1966   "Non-Thematic Subjects in Contemporary English", *Tra-
           vaux linguistiques de Prague* 2: 239–56.
    1968   "On the Prosodic Features of the Modern English Finite
           Verb as a Means of Functional Sentence Perspective", *Brno
           Studies in English* 7: 11–48.
Firth, J. R.
    1957   *Papers in Linguistics, 1934–1951* (London: Oxford University
           Press).

Fishman, Joshua *et alii*
    c1966 *Language Loyalty in the United States, the Maintenance and
           Perpetuation of Non-English Mother Tongues by American
           Ethnic and religious Groups* (= *Janua Linguarum, series
           maior* 21) (London – The Hague – Paris: Mouton & Co.).
Flydal, Leif
    1952   "Remarques sur certains rapports entre le style et l'état de
           langue", *Norsk tidsskrift for sprogvidenskap* 16: 241–58.

Fodor, Jerry A. – Jerrold J. Katz (eds.)
    c1964 *The Structure of Language; Readings in the Philosophy of
           Language* (Englewood Cliffs, N. J.: Prentice-Hall Inc.).

Fowler, Roger (ed.)
    c1966 *Essays on Style and Language* (London: Routledge – Kegan
           Paul).

Fowler, Roger – Peter Mercer
    1969   "Criticism and the Language of Literature: Some Traditions
           and Trends in Great Britain", *Style* 3: 45–72.

Freeman, Donald C. (ed.)
    c1970 *Linguistics and Literary Style* (New York, etc.: Holt, Rinehart
           and Winston Inc.).
Fries, Charles Carpenter
    1940   *American English Grammar* (New York: Appleton-Century-
           Crofts).
    1952   *The Structure of English; an Introduction to the Construction
           of English Sentences* (New York: Harcourt, Brace & World).

Fucks, Wilhelm
1955 *Mathematische Analyse von Sprachelementen, Sprachstil und Sprachen* (= *Arbeitsgemeinschaft für Forschung des Landes Nordrhein–Westfalen* 34 A) (Köln–Opladen: Westdeutscher Verlag).
Gal'perin, I. R.
1958 *Očerki po stilistike anglijskogo jazyka* [Notes on the stylistics of English] (= *Biblioteka filologa*) (Moskva: Izdatel'stvo literatury na inostrannyx jazykax).
1967 "Javljaetsja li stilistika urovnem jazyka?" [Is stylistics a level of language?] in: *Problemy jazykoznanija. Doklady i soobščenija sovetskix učenyx na X Meždunarodnom kongresse lingvistov (Bukarest, 28.8. – 2.9. 1967)* (Reds.: F. P. Filin, B. A. Serebrennikov, *et alii*) (Moskva: Izdatel'stvo Nauka), pp. 198–202.
1968 *An Essay in Stylistic Analysis* (Moskva: Izdatel'stvo Nauka).
1971 "Some Principal Issues of Style and Stylistics as Viewed by Russian Linguists", *Style* 5: 1–20.
Gal'perin, I. R. (ed.)
c1969 *Naučnaja konferencija problemy lingvističeskoj stilistiki* [A scientific conference on problems of linguistic stylistics] (Moskva: Ministerstvo vysšego i srednego special'nogo obrazovanija SSSR).
Garvin, Paul L. (ed.)
c1964 *A Prague School Reader on Esthetics, Literary Structure, and Style* (Washington, D. C.: Georgetown University Press).
Genung, John Franklin
1900 *The Working Principles of Rhetoric* (Boston etc.: Ginn and Company).
Gibson, Walker
1966 *Tough, Sweet and Stuffy; an Essay on Modern American Prose Styles* (Bloomington – London: Indiana University Press).
Ginzburg, R.
1969 "On Some Trends in Stylistic Research", *Style* 3: 73–90.
Gläser, Rosemarie
1963 "Neuwörter im politischen Englisch", *Zeitschrift für Anglistik und Amerikanistik* 11: 229–47.
1970a "Sprache und Pragmatik der englisch-amerikanischen kommerziellen Werbung", *Zeitschrift für Anglistik und Amerikanistik* 18: 314–23.
1970b *Thesen zur Habilitationsschrift 'Linguistische Kriterien der Stilbeschreibung'* (University of Leipzig). [typescript]
1970c "Extratextuale Faktoren der Stilbeschreibung", *Wissen-*

*schaftliche Zeitschrift der Pädagogischen Hochschule "Dr.
Theodor Neubauer" Erfurt/Mühlhausen, Gesellschafts- und
sprachwissenschaftliche Reihe* 7.2: 89–91.

Gopnik, Irwin
  1970   *A Theory of Style and Richardson's Clarissa (= De propietati-
          bus litterarum, series practica* 10) (The Hague– Paris: Mouton).

Gordon, Ian A.
  1966   *The Movement of English Prose* (London: Longmans, Green
          and Co. Ltd.).

Gorrell, Robert M. (ed.)
  c1967   *Rhetoric: Theories for Application* (Champaign, Ill.: National
          Council of Teachers of English).

Gougenheim, G.
  1959   "La statistique de vocabulaire", *Revue de l'enseignement
          supérieur* 1959.1: 137–44.

Grahn, Lars
  1965   "Det moderna tidningsspråket" [Modern newspaper lan-
          guage], *Språkvård* 4: 3–11.

Graur, A. *et alii* (eds.)
  c1970   *Actes du 10ᵉ Congrès International des Linguistes,* 4 vol. (Buca-
          rest: Editions de l'Academie de la République Socialiste de
          Roumanie).

Gray, Bennison
  1969   *Style; the Problem and Its Solution (= De proprietatibus
          litterarum, series maior* 3) (The Hague: Mouton).

Greenbaum, Sidney – Randolph Quirk
  1970   *Elicitation Experiments in English; Linguistic Studies in Use
          and Attitude* (London: Longman Group Ltd.).

Gregory, Michael
  1967   "Aspects of Varieties Differentiation", *Journal of Linguistics*
          3: 177–98.

Greimas, A. J.
  1966   *Sémantique structurale; recherche de méthode (= Langue et
          langage)* (Paris: Librairie Larousse).

Guilbert, Louis
  1965   *La formation du vocabulaire d'aviation (1861–1891)* (Paris:
          Larousse).
  1967   *Le vocabulaire de l'astronautique (= Publications de l'Uni-
          versité de Rouen, Faculté des Lettres et Sciences Humaines)*
          (Paris: Larousse).

Guiraud, Pierre
  1954   *Les caractères statistiques du vocabulaire* (Paris: Presses Uni-
          versitaires de France).

1959   *Problèmes et methodes de la statistique linguistique* (Dordrecht:
       D. Reidel Publishing Company).
1963   *La stylistique (= Que sais-je?* 646) (Paris: Presses Universi-
       taires de France).
Guiraud, Pierre – Paul Zumthor – A. Kibedi Varga – J. A. G. Tans
1962   *Style et littèrature* (La Haye: Van Goor Zonen).
Gumperz, John J.
1964   "Speech Variation and the Study of Indian Civilization"
       in HYMES (1964: 416–28).
Hallberg, Peter
1962   *Snorri Sturluson och Egils Saga Skallagrimssonar; ett försök
       till språklig författarbestämning* [Snorri Sturluson and the
       saga of Egil Skallagrimsson; an attempt at linguistic deter-
       mination of authorship] *(= Studia Islandica* 20) (Reykja-
       vìk: Heimspekideild Háskóla Islands og Bókaútgáfa Men-
       ningarsjóds).
1963   *Ólafr þórdarson Hvitaskáld, Knytlinga Saga och Laxdœla Saga;
       ett försök till språklig författarbestämning* [Ólafr þórdarson
       Hvitaskáld, Knytlinga Saga, and Laxdæla Saga; an attempt
       at linguistic determination of authorship] *(= Studia Islandi-
       ca* 22) (Reykjavík: Heimspekideild Háskóla Islands og Bóka-
       útgáfa Menningarsjóds).
1968   *Stilsignalement och författarskap i norrön sagalitteratur; syn-
       punkter och exempel* [Stylistic features and authorship in
       Nordic saga literature; viewpoints and examples] *(= Acta
       Universitatis Gothoburgensis, Nordica Gothoburgensia* 3)
       (Stockholm, etc.: Almqvist and Wiksell).
Hallberg, Peter *et alii*
c1966 *Litteraturvetenskap; nya mål och metoder* [The study of litera-
       ture; new goals and methods] (Stockholm: Natur och
       Kultur).
Halliday, M. A. K.
1967–68 "Notes on Transitivity and Theme in English", *Journal of
       Linguistics* 3: 37–81, 199–244; 4: 179–215.
Hamilton, Sir George Rostrevor
1949   *The Tell-Tale Article; a Critical Approach to Modern Poetry*
       (London, etc.: Heinemann).
Harris, Zellig
1952a "Discourse Analysis", *Language* 28: 1–30.
1952b "Discourse Analysis: A Sample Text", *Language* 28: 474–94.
Harweg, Roland
1968   *Pronomina und Textkonstitution* (= *Beiheft zu Poetica*
       2) (München: Wilhelm Fink Verlag).

Hasan, Ruqaiya
  1968 *Grammatical Cohesion in Spoken and Written English* 1
         (= Programme in Linguistics and English Teaching 7) (Lon-
         don: Longmans).
Hayes, Curtis W.
  1968 "A Transformational-Generative Approach to Style: Samuel
         Johnson and Edward Gibbon", *Language and Style* 1: 39-48.
Hendricks, W. O.
  1968 "On the Notion 'Beyond the Sentence'", *Linguistics* 37:
         12-51.
  1969 "Three Models for the Description of Poetry", *Journal of
         Linguistics* 5: 1-22.
Herdan, Gustav
  1956 *Language as Choice and Chance* (Groningen: Noordhoff).
  1960 *Type-Token Mathematics (= Janua Linguarum, series maior*
         4) (The Hague: Mouton).
  1962 *The Calculus of Linguistic Observations (= Janua Linguarum,
         series maior* 9) (The Hague: Mouton).
  1964a *Quantitative Linguistics* (London: Butterworths).
  1964b "On Communication between Linguists", *Linguistics* 9: 71-6.
  1966 *The Advanced Theory of Language as Choice and Chance* (Ber-
         lin, etc.: Springer Verlag).
  1969 "The Jig-Saw Puzzle of Saussurian and Quantitative Lin-
         guistics", *Lingua e stile* 4: 69-76.
Hill, Archibald A.
  1958 *Introduction to Linguistic Structures; from Sound to Sentence
         in English* (New York: Harcourt Brace & Co.).
  1964 "The Locus of the Literary Work", in: *English Studies Today;
         Third Series* (Ed.: G. J. Duthie) (Edinburgh: University
         Press), pp. 41-50.
  1965 *Essays in Literary Analysis* (Austin, Tex.). [a collection of
         fourteen mimeographed or xeroxed, previously published
         articles]
Hill, Archibald A. (ed.)
  c1953 *Report on the Fourth Annual Round Table Meeting on Lingu-
         istics and Language Teaching* (Washington, D. C.: Georgetown
         University Press).
Hough, Graham
  1969 *Style and Stylistics* (London: Routledge – Kegan Paul; New
         York: Humanities Press).
Hymes, Dell (ed.)
  c1964 *Language in Culture and Society; a Reader in Linguistics and
         Anthropology* (New York: Harper – Row).

Ikegami, Yoshihiko
1969 "A Linguistic Essay on Parody", *Linguistics* 55: 13–31.
Jacobs, Roderick A. – Peter S. Rosenbaum
c1970 *Readings in English Transformational Grammar* (Waltham, Mass. – Toronto – London: Ginn Co.).
Jakobson, Roman
1960 "Linguistics and Poetics" in SEBEOK (1960: 350–77).
Jelínek, J. – J. V. Vecka – M. Tešitelova
1961 *Frekvence slov, slovních druhů a tvarů v ceském jazyce* [The frequency of words, word combinations and idioms in Czech] (Praha: Československa Akademie Věd).
Johannet, José
1963 "Le style nominal en russe dans la langue administrative du 18ᵉ siècle", *Revue des Études Slaves* 42: 97–107.
Joos, Martin
1962 *The Five Clocks (= Publications of Indiana University Research Center in Anthropology, Folklore, and Linguistics 22, = International Journal of American Linguistics 28.2.)* (Bloomington, Ind.: Indiana University; The Hague: Mouton & Co.).
Jörgensen, Nils
1971 *Om makrosyntagmer i informell och formell stil (= Lundastudier i nordisk språkvetenskap C.3)* (Lund: Studentlitteratur).
Josselson, H. H.
1953 *The Russian Word Count and Frequency Analysis of Grammatic Categories of Standard Literary Russian* (Detroit: Wayne State University Press).
Juilland, A. – E. Chang-Rodriguez
1964 *Frequency Dictionary of Spanish Words (= The Romance Languages and Their Structures S1)* (The Hague: Mouton).
Juilland, A. – P. M. H. Edwards – I. Juilland
1965 *Frequency Dictionary of Rumanian Words (= The Romance Languages and Their Structures R1)* (The Hague: Mouton).
Kaeding, F. W.
1898 *Häufigkeitswörterbuch der deutschen Sprache, festgestellt durch einen Arbeitsausschuss der deutschen Stenographiesysteme* (Steglitz: Mittler). [reprint: (New York: The Macmillan Company 1928)]
Kaluža, Irena
1967 *The Functioning of Sentence Structure in the Stream-of-Consciousness Technique of William Faulkner's 'The Sound and the Fury'; a Study in Linguistic Stylistics (= Prace Historycz-*

no-literackie 13) (Kraków: Zeszytu Naukowe Universytetu Jagiellonskiego CLVI).

Kaplan, Abraham
  1964 *The Conduct of Inquiry; Methodology for Behavioral Science* (San Francisco: Chandler Publishing Co.).

Karlsen, Rolf
  1959 *Studies in the Connection of Clauses in Current English* (Bergen: J. W. Eides Boktrykkeri A. S.).

Karvonen, Juhani *et alii*
  1970 *Opettajan sanastokirja* [A teacher's word-book] (Jyväskylä: K. J. Gummerus Osakeyhtiö).

Kayser, Wolfgang
  1948 *Das sprachliche Kunstwerk* (Bern: Francke).

Kiefer, Ferenc
  1967 *On Emphasis and Word Order in Hungarian* (= *Indiana University Publications, Uralic and Altaic Series* 76) (Bloomington: Indiana University; The Hague: Mouton).

Kiefer, Ferenc (ed.)
  c1969 *Studies in Syntax and Semantics* (= *Foundations of Language, Supplementary Series* 10) (Dordrecht: D. Reidel Publishing Company).

Kinnander, Bengt
  1959 *Sammanhangsanalys; studier i språkets struktur och rytm* [Context analysis; studies in the structure and rhythm of language] (= *Skrifter utgivna av Institutionen för nordiska språk vid Uppsala Universitet* 5) (Uppsala: Almqvist & Wiksell).

Kiparsky, Paul
  1968 "Linguistic Universals and Linguistic Change" in BACH – HARMS (1968: 171–202).

Klein, Sheldon
  1965 "Control of Style with a Generative Grammar", *Language* 41: 619–31.

Kloepfer, Rolf – Ursula Oomen
  1970 *Sprachliche Konstituenten moderner Dichtung; Entwurf einer deskriptiven Poetik. Rimbaud* (Bad Homburg: Athenäum Verlag).

Koch, Walter A.
  1966 *Recurrence and a Three-Modal Approach to Poetry* (= *De proprietatibus litterarum, series minor* 2) (The Hague: Mouton).
  1970 "Zur Ablesbarkeit von Mustern von Textanalysen" in GRAUR (1970 3: 389–93).

Kondrašov, N. A. (ed.)
  c1967 *Pražskij lingvističeskij kružok; sbornik statej* [The Linguistic

Circle of Prague; a collection of articles] (Moskva: Izdatel'stvo Progress).

Kovtunova, I. I.
1969 *Porjadok slov v russkom literaturnom jazyke XVIII — pervoj treti XIX v. Puti stanovlenija sovremennoj normy* [Word order in the Russian literary language of the 18th and the first third of the 19th century; the development of the modern norm] (Moskva: Izdatel'stvo Nauka).

Kraus, Jiři – Josef Polák
1967 "Text Factors and Characteristics", *Prague Studies in Mathematical Linguistics* 2: 155–71.

Kreuzer, Helmut – Rul Gunzenhäuser (eds.)
c1967 *Mathematik und Dichtung (= Sammlung Dialog 3)* (München: Nymphenburger Verlagshandlung).

Kučera, Henry – W. Nelson Francis
1967 *Computational Analysis of Present-Day American English* (Providence, R. I.: Brown University Press).

Labov, William
1966 *The Social Stratification of English in New York City* (Washington, D. C.: Center for Applied Linguistics).
1969 "Contraction, Deletion, and Inherent Variability of the English Copula", *Language* 15: 715–62.

Labov, William – Joshua Waletzky
1967 "Narrative Analysis: Oral Versions of Personal Experience", in: *Essays on the Verbal and Visual Arts: Proceedings of the 1966 Annual Spring Meeting of the American Ethnological Society* (Ed.: J. Holm) (Seattle, Wash.: University of Washington Press).

Lakoff, George P.
1969 "On Generative Semantics", in: *Semantics; an Interdisciplinary Reader* (Ed.: D. D. Steinberg — L. A. Jakobovits). (London: Cambridge University Press).

Lamb, Sidney M.
1966 *Outline of Stratificational Grammar* (Washington, D. C.: Georgetown University Press).

Lambert, W. E.
1967 "The Use of *Tu* and *Vous* as Forms of Address in French Canada: A Pilot Study", *Journal of Verbal Learning and Verbal Behavior* 6: 614–7.

Leech, Geoffrey N.
1966 *English in Advertising; a Linguistic Study of Advertising in Great Britain* (London: Longmans, Green & Co., Ltd.).

1969 *A Linguistic Guide to English Poetry* (London: Longmans, Green & Co, Ltd.).

Leed, Jacob (ed.)

c1966 *The Computer and Literary Style* (Kent, Ohio: Kent State University Press).

Leont'ev A. A.

1968 "Issledovanija poetičeskoj reči" [The study of poetic speech], in: *Teoretičeskie problemy sovetskogo jazykoznanija* (Moskva: Izdatel'stvo Nauka).

Lesskis, G. A.

1964 "O zavisimosti meždu razmerom predloženija i ego strukturoj v raznyx vidax teksta" [The relationship between sentence length and sentence structure in various types of text], *Voprosy jazykoznanija* 3.3: 99–123.

Levin, Samuel R.

1963 "Deviation — Statistical and Determinate — in Poetic Language", *Lingua* 12: 276–90.

1965a "Internal and External Deviation in Poetry", *Word* 21: 225–37.

1965b "Langage and Parole in American Linguistics", *Foundations of Language* 1: 83–94.

Lodge, David

c1966 *Language of Fiction; Essays in Criticism and Verbal Analysis of the English Novel* (London: Routledge & Kegan Paul; New York: Columbia University Press).

Loman, Bengt

1970 "Social Variation in the Syntax of Spoken Swedish" in BENEDIKTSSON (1970: 211–34).

Loman, Bengt – Nils Jörgensen

1971 *Manual för analys och beskrivning av makrosyntagmer* (= *Lundastudier i nordisk språkvetenskap* C.1) (Lund: Studentlitteratur).

Longacre, Robert E.

1970 "Sentence Structure as a Statement Calculus", *Language* 46: 783–815.

Lott, Bernard

1960 *Style and Linguistics; an Inaugural Lecture* (Djakarta: Penerbit Djambatan).

Love, Glen A. – Michael Payne (eds.)

c1969 *Contemporary Essays on Style* (Glenview, Ill.: Scott–Foresman & Company).

Lunt, Horace G. (ed.)

c1964 *Proceedings of the Ninth International Congress of Linguists,*

Cambridge, Mass., August 27–31, 1962 (= Janua Linguarum, series maior 12) (London – The Hague – Paris: Mouton & Co.)

Malblanc, Alfred
1961 *Stylistique comparée du français et de l'allemand* (Paris – Bruxelles: Didier).

Mandelbrot, Benoit
1954 "Structure formelle des textes et communication", *Word* 10: 1–27.

Marcus, Solomon
1970 *Poetica matematica* (Bucureşti: Editura Academiei Republicii Socialiste Romania).

Marouzeau, Jules
1946a *Précis de stylistique française* (Paris: Masson).
1946b *Traité de stylistique latine* (Paris: Les belles lettres).

Martin, Harold C. (ed.)
c1959 *Style in Prose Fiction; English Institute Essays 1958* (New York – London: Columbia University Press.).

McCawley, James D.
1968 "Concerning the Base Component of a Transformational Grammar", *Foundations of Language* 4: 243–69.

McIntosh, Angus
1965 "Saying", *Review of English Literature* 6: 9–20.

McKinnon, Alastair – Roger Webster
1969 "A Method of Author Identification", *Computer Studies in the Humanities and Verbal Behaviour* 2: 19–23.

Mathesius, Vilém
c1947 *Čeština a obecny jazykozpyt, soubor stati* [Czech and General Linguistics; a collection of papers] (Praha: Melantrich).

Meetham, A. R. – R. A. Hudson (eds.)
c1969 *Encyclopaedia of Linguistics, Information, and Control* (Oxford, etc.: Pergamon Press).

Meier, H.
1967 *Deutsche Sprachstatistik*[3] (Hildesheim: Olms). [1st edition (1964)]

Mel'čuk, I. A. – A. K. Žolkovskij
1970 "Towards a Functioning 'Meaning-Text' Model of Language", *Linguistics* 57: 10–47.

Mihailescu–Urechia, Venera
1970 "Are Novelists Free to Choose Their Own Style?", *Linguistics* 59: 37–61.

Miles, Josephine
1960 *Renaissance, Eighteenth-Century, and Modern Language in*

English Poetry; a Tabular View (Berkeley, Cal.: University of California Press).

1964 *Eras and Modes in English Poetry* (Berkeley, Cal.: University of California Press).

1965 *The Continuity of Poetic Language*, 3 vol. (New York: Octagon Books Inc.).

1967 *Style and Proportion; the Language of Prose and Poetry* (Boston: Little – Brown).

Milic, Louis T.

1967 *A Quantitative Approach to the Style of Jonathan Swift* (= *Studies in English Literature* 23) (The Hague: Mouton).

c1969 *Stylists on Style; a Handbook with Selections for Analysis* (New York: Charles Scribner's Sons).

Miller, G. R. – E. B. Coleman

1967 "A Set of Thirty-Six Prose Passages Calibrated for Complexity", *Journal of Verbal Learning and Verbal Behavior* 6: 851-4.

Mistrik, Josef

1967 "Matematiko-statističeskie metody v stilistike" [Mathematical-statistic methods in stylistics], *Voprosy jazykoznanija* 16.3: 42–52.

1969 *Frekvencia slov v slovenčine* [Word frequency in Slovak] (Bratislava: Vydavatelstvo Slovanskej Akadémie Vied).

Modéer, Ivar

1952 *Utlåtande om professorerna Erik Wellanders och Ture Johannissons utredning rörande författarskapet till vissa anonyma brev* [Remarks on the statements of professors Erik Wellander and Ture Johannisson concerning the authorship of certain anonymous letters] (Uppsala: Lundequistska bokhandeln).

Moerk, Ernst L.

1970 "Quantitative Analysis of Writing Styles", *Journal of Linguistics* 6: 223–30.

Morton, A. Q.

1965 "The Authorship of the Pauline Epistles: A Scientific Approach", *Journal of the Royal Statistical Society* 128: 169.

Mosteller, Frederick – David L. Wallace

1963 "Inference in an Authorship Problem", *Journal of the American Statistical Association* 58: 275–309.

1964 *Inference and Disputed Authorship: The Federalist* (Reading, Mass.: Addison–Wesley Publishing Company, Inc.).

Mounin, Georges

1963 *Les problèmes théoriques de la traduction* (Paris: Editions Gallimard).

Mourot, J.
1964 "Stylistique des intentions et stylistique des effets", *CAIEF* 16: 71–9.

Muller, Charles
1968 *Initiation à la statistique linguistique* (= *Langue et langage*) (Paris: Librairie Larousse).

Mundt, Marina
1969 *Sturla Þórdarson und die Laxdaela Saga* (Bergen, etc.: Universitetsforlaget).

Naert, Pierre
1949 *Stilen i Vilhelm Ekelunds aforismer och essäer* [The style in Vilhelm Ekelund's aphorisms and essays] (Lund: Gleerup).

Nickel, Gerhard
1970 "Some Contextual Relations between Sentences in English" in GRAUR (1970 2: 877–84).

Nida, Eugene A.
1964 *Toward a Science of Translating; with Special Reference to Principles and Procedures Involved in Bible Translating* (Leiden: Brill).

Nikolaev, P. A.
1968 *Teorija stilja* [A theory of style] (Moskva: Iskusstvo).

Nowottny, Winifred
1962 *The Language Poets Use* (London: The Athlone Press).

Ohmann, Richard M.
1962 *Shaw; the Style and the Man* (Middletown, Conn.: Wesleyan University Press).
1964 "Generative Grammars and the Concept of Literary Style", *Word* 20: 423–39.
1966 "Literature as Sentences" in CHATMAN–LEVIN (1967: 231–8).

Osselton, N. E.
1958 *Branded Words in English Dictionaries before Johnson* (= *Groningen Studies in English* 7) (Groningen: J. B. Wolters).

Pasini, Gian Franco
1968 "Lo studio delle metafore", *Lingua e stile* 3: 71–89.

Petőfi, Janos S.
1970 *Von der 'Explikation des Begriffes Satz' zu der 'Explikation der Texte'; zur Frage einer generellen Texttheorie* (Göteborg: Göteborgs Universitet, Forskningsgruppen för modern svenska, Språkdata). [mimeographed]

Pike, Kenneth L.
1967 *Language in Relation to a Unified Theory of the Structure of Human Behavior* (= *Janua Linguarum, series maior* 24) (The Hague: Mouton).

Posner, Rebecca
  1963   "The Use and Abuse of Stylistic Statistics", *Archivum Linguisticum* 15: 111–39.
Propp, Vladimir
  1958   *Morphology of the Folktale*, translated by Laurence Scott (The Hague: Mouton).
Quadlbauer, Franz
  1962   *Die antike Theorie der* genera dicendi *im lateinischen Mittelalter* (= *Sitzungsberichte der Oesterreichischen Akademie der Wissenschaften, philosophisch-historische Klasse* 241.2) (Graz etc.: H. Böhlaus Nachfolger).
Quirk, Randolph
  1968   *Essays on the English Language, Medieval and Modern* (London: Longmans).
Quirk, Randolph – Jan Svartvik
  1966   *Investigating Linguistic Acceptability* (= *Janua Linguarum, series minor* 54) (The Hague: Mouton).
Reibel, David A. – Sanford A. Schane (eds.)
  c1969   *Modern Studies in English; Readings in Transformational Grammar* (Englewood Cliffs, N. J.: Prentice-Hall Inc.).
Riffaterre, Michael
  1959   "Criteria for Style Analysis", *Word* 15: 154–74.
  1960   "Stylistic Context", *Word* 16: 207–18.
  1961a "Problemes d'analyse du style littéraire", *Romance Philology* 14: 216–27.
  1961b "Vers la définition du style", *Word* 17: 318–44.
  1964   "The Stylistic Function" in Lunt (1964: 316–23).
Rosengren, Karl Erik
  1968   *Sociological Aspects of the Literary System* (Stockholm: Natur och Kultur).
Rosiello, Luigi
  1965   *Struttura, uso e funzioni della lingua* (Firenze: Vallecchi).
Ross, John
  1970   "On Declarative Sentences" in Jacobs – Rosenbaum (1970: 222–72).
Runquist, C. – G.
  1958   *Ett falskt kombinationslås; språkutredningen i Helandermålet* [A false combination-lock; the linguistic investigation in the Helander case] (Stockholm: Seelig).
Šajkevič, A. Ja.
  1968   "Opyt statističeskogo vydelenija functional'nyx stilej" [An attempt at the statistical determination of functional styles], *Voprosy jazykoznanija* 7.1 : 64–76.

Šaumjan, S. K.
1965   *Strukturnaja lingvistika* [Structural linguistics] (Moskva: Izdatel'stvo Nauka).

de Saussure, Ferdinand
1955   *Cours de linguistique générale* [5] (Ed.: Charles Bally and Albert Sechehaye with the collaboration of Albert Riedlinger) (Paris: Payot).

Sayce, R. A.
1953   *Style in French Prose* (Oxford: Basil Blackwell).
1962   "The Definition of the Term Style", in: *Actes du 3ᵉ Congrès de l'Association Internationale de Littérature Comparée, Utrecht, 1961* (The Hague: Mouton), pp. 156–66.

Sebeok, Thomas A. (ed.)
c1960   *Style in Language* (Cambridge, Mass.: The M. I. T. Press).

Sebeok, Thomas A. – Alfred S. Hayes – May Catherine Bateson (eds.)
c1964   *Approaches to Semiotics: Cultural Anthropology, Education, Linguistics, Psychiatry, Psychology (= Janua Linguarum, series maior* 15) (The Hague: Mouton).

Sedelow, Sally Yates
1965–67 *Stylistic Analysis; Reports on the First, Second, and Third Years of Research* (Santa Monica, Cal.: Systems Development Corporation).

Sedelow, Sally Yates – Walter A. Sedelow
1966   "A Preface to Computational Stylistics" in LEEDS (1966: 1–13).

Segre, Cesare
1968   *Lingua, stile e società* (Roma: Feltrinelli).

Sgall, Petr
1969   "L'ordre des mots et la sémantique" in KIEFER (1969: 231–40).

Sil'man, T. I.
1967   *Problemy sintaksičeskoj stilistiki (na materiale nemeckoj prozy)* [Problems of syntactic stylistics, on the basis of German prose] (= *Leningradskij ordena trudovogo krasnogo znameni gosudarstvennyj pedagogičeskij institut imeni A. I. Gercena, Učenye zapiski* 315) (Leningrad: Prosveščenie).

Sinclair, John McH.
1968   "A Technique of Stylistic Description", *Language and Style* 1: 215–42.

Slama-Cazacu, Tatiana
1961   *Langage et contexte. Le problème du langage dans la conception de l'expression et de l'interprétation par des organisations contextuelles (= Janua Linguarum, series maior* 6) (The Hague: Mouton).

Somers, H. H.
1959 *Analyse mathématique du langage* (Louvain: Nauwelaerts).
1967 *Analyse statistique du style* (Louvain – Paris: Nauwelaerts).
Spevack, Marvin
1968–70 *A Complete and Systematic Concordance to the Works of Shakespeare*, 6 vol. (Hildesheim: Georg Olms).
Spitzer, Leo
1948 *Linguistics and Literary History; Essays in Stylistics* (Princeton, N. J.: Princeton University Press).
1961 *Stilstudien*[2], 2 vol. (München: Hueber). [1: *Sprachstile;* 2: *Stilsprachen*]
Statsrådsberedningen (G. E., B. M.)
1967 *Språket i lagar och andra författningar* [The language of laws and other statutes] (Stockholm: Svenska Reproduktions AB).
Štejnfel'dt, E. A.
1963 *Častotnyj slovar' sovremennogo russkogo literaturnogo jazyka* [A frequency dictionary of modern literary Russian] (Tallinn: Naučno-issledovatel'skij institut pedagogiki Éstonskoj SSR).
Stempel, Wolf-Dieter (ed.)
1971 *Beiträge zur Textlinguistik* (= *Internationale Bibliothek für allgemeine Linguistik* 1) (München: Wilhelm Fink Verlag).
Stone, P. J. et *alii*
1966 *The General Inquirer; a Computer Approach to Content Analysis* (Cambridge, Mass. — London: The M. I. T. Press).
Straumann, Heinrich
1935 *Newspaper Headlines; a Study in Linguistic Method* (London: G. Allen & Unwin Ltd.).
Striedter, Jurij, (ed.)
c1969 *Texte der russischen Formalisten* 1 (München: Wilhelm Fink Verlag).
Svartvik, Jan
1968 *The Evans Statements; a Case for Forensic Linguistics* (= *Gothenburg Studies in English* 20) (Stockholm: Almquist — Wiksell).
Swieczkowski, Valerian
1961 "On the Margin of Syntax and Style", in: *Poetics. Poetyka. Poètika* 1 (Eds.: D. Davie, I. Fonagy, R. Jakobson et *alii*) (Warszawa: Panstwowe Wydawnictwo Naukowe; 's-Gravenhage: Mouton), pp. 463–9.
Tatilon, Claude
1970 "Les grandes options de la stylistique littéraire", *Le Français dans le monde* 71: 10–6.

Teleman, Ulf – Anne Marie Wieselgren
  1970 *ABC i stilistik* [ABC of stylistics] (Lund: Gleerup).
Tenow, Nore
  1963 *De anonyma breven i Helandermålet* [The anonymous letters in the Helander case] (Stockholm: Forum).
Terracini, Benventuno
  1968 *Analisi stilistici; teoria, storia, problemi* (Milano: Feltrinelli).
Thesleff, Holger
  1967 *Studies in the Styles of Plato (= Acta Philosophica Fennica* 20) (Helsinki: Societas Philosophica Fennica).
Thorndike, E. L.— I. Lorge
  1944 *The Teacher's Word Book of 30,000 Words* (New York: Columbia University Teachers College Bureau of Publications).
Thorne, J. P.
  1965 "Stylistics and Generative Grammars", *Journal of Linguistics* 1: 49–59.
  1969 "Poetry, Stylistics, and Imaginary Grammars", *Journal of Linguistics* 5: 147–50.
  1970 "Generative Grammar and Stylistic Analysis", in: *New Horizons in Linguistics* (Ed.: John Lyons) (Harmondsworth, Middlesex: Penguin Books Ltd.), pp. 185–97.
Todd, M. J.
  1969 "Newspaper Style; a Practical Investigation", *English Language Teaching* 23: 138–41.
Todorov, Tzvetan
  c1965 *Théorie de la litterature; textes des formalistes russes* (Paris: Editions Seuil).
Traugott, Elizabeth Closs
  1965 "Diachronic Syntax and Generative Grammar", *Language* 41: 402–15.
Uitti, Karl D.
  1969 *Linguistics and Literary Theory* (Englewood Cliffs, N. J.: Prentice-Hall).
Ullmann, Stephen
  1964a *Language and Style* (Oxford: Basil Blackwell).
  1964b *Style in the French Novel* (London: Cambridge University Press).
Ure, Jean
  1968 "Practical Registers", *English Language Teaching* 22: 107–14.
Vachek, Josef (ed.)
  c1964 *A Prague School Reader in Linguistics* (Bloomington, Ind.: Indiana University Press).
  c1966 *Dictionnaire de linguistique de l'Ecole de Prague* (Utrecht: Amvers).

Vander Beke, G. E.
1929 *French Word Book* (New York: The Macmillan Co.).
Vinay, Jean-Paul – Jean-Louis Darbelnet
1964 *Stylistique comparée du français et de l'anglais* (Paris – Bruxelles: Didier).
Vinogradov, V. V.
1961 *Problema avtorstva i teorija stilej* [The problem of authorship and the theory of style] (Moskva: Izdatel'stvo Akademii Nauk SSSR).
1963a *Sjužet i stil'* [Subject and style] (Moskva: Izdatel'stvo Akademii Nauk SSSR).
1963b *Stilistika; teorija poetičeskoj reči; poètika* [Stylistics; theory of poetic (Izdatel'stvo Akademii Nauk SSSR).
Vinogradov, V. V. – V. G. Kostomarov
1967 "Teorija sovetskogo jazykoznanija i praktika obučenija russkomu jazyku inostrancev" [The theory of Soviet linguistics and the practice of the teaching of Russian to foreigners], *Voprosy jazykoznanija* 17.2: 3–17.
Vomperskij, V. P. (ed.)
c1966 *Voprosy stilistiki, sbornik statej k 70-letiju so dnja roždenija [. . .] K. I. Bylinskogo* [Problems of stylistics; a collection of articles on the occasion of the 70th birthday of K. I. Bylinskij] (Moskva: Izdatel'stvo Moskovskogo Universiteta).
Vossler, Karl
1913 *Frankreichs Kultur im Spiegel seiner Sprachentwicklung* (Heidelberg: Carl Winter).
1923 *Gesammelte Aufsätze zur Sprachphilosophie* (München: M. Hueber).
Wängler, H. H.
1963 *Rangwörterbuch hochdeutscher Umgangssprache* (Marburg: Elwert).
Warburg, Jeremy
1959 "Some Aspects of Style", in: *The Teaching of English* (= *Studies in Communications* 3) (Ed.: Randolph Quirk – A. H. Smith) (London: Secker – Warburg), pp. 36–59.
1965 "Idiosyncratic Style", *Review of English Literature* 6: 56–65.
Wartburg, Walther von
1969 *Problems and Methods in Linguistics*, revised edition with the collaboration of Stephen Ullmann, translated by Joyce M. H. Reid (Oxford: Basil Blackwell).
Weinrich, Harald
1964 *Tempus; besprochene und erzählte Welt* (Stuttgart: Kohlhammer).

1966   *Linguistik der Lüge* (Heidelberg: L. Schneider).

Weisgerber, Leo
1953–54 *Von der Kräften der deutschen Sprache*, 2 vol. (Düsseldorf: Schwann). [1: *Die inhaltsbezogene Grammatik*; 2: *Die sprachliche Erschliessung der Welt*]

Wellek, René – Austin Warren
1949   *Theory of Literature* (New York: Harcourt, Brace & Co.).

Wexler, Peter J.
1955   *La formation du vocabulaire des chemins de fer en France (1778–1842)* (Genève: Droz).

Wiio, Osmo A.
1968   *Readability, Comprehension and Readership* (= *Acta Universitatis Tamperensis* 22) (Tampere: Tampereen Yliopisto).

Williams, C. B.
1970   *Style and Vocabulary: Numerical Studies* (London: Griffin).

Wimsatt, W. K., Jr.
1941   *The Prose Style of Samuel Johnson* (New Haven: Yale University Press).
1954   *The Verbal Icon* (Lexington, Kent.: University of Kentucky Press).

Winburne, John Newton
1964   "Sentence Sequence in Discourse" in LUNT (1964: 1094–9).

Winter, Werner
1961   "Relative Häufigkeit syntaktischer Erscheinungen als Mittel zur Abgrenzung von Stilarten", *Phonetica* 7: 193–216.
1964   "Styles as Dialects" in LUNT (1964: 324–30).

Yngve, Victor H.
1960   "A Model and a Hypothesis for Language Structure", *Proceedings of the American Philosophical Society* 104: 444–66.

Yule, G. Udny
1938   "On Sentence-Length as a Statistical Characteristic of Style in Prose", *Biometrika* 30: 363–90.
1944   *The Statistical Study of Literary Vocabulary* (Cambridge: Cambridge University Press).

Ziff, Paul
1964   "On Understanding 'Understanding Utterances' " in FODOR – KATZ (1964: 390–9).

Zimmermann, Heinz
1965   *Zu einer Typologie des spontanen Gesprächs; syntaktische Studien zur baseldeutschen Umgangssprache* (= *Basler Studien zur deutschen Sprache und Literatur* 30) (Bern: Francke).

Zipf, George Kingsley

    1949 *Human Behavior and the Principle of Least Effort* (Cambridge, Mass.: Addison–Wesley).

    1965 *The Psycho-Biology of Language; an Introduction to Dynamic Philology*[2] (Cambridge, Mass.: The M. I. T. Press).

11

INDEX TO REFERENCES